Dear li
Thanks re
taking an interest in
my project!
Sondra Dindle

sdundle@bell.net

Eyes Wide Open

Eyes Wide Open

A Mother and Daughter's Unbelievable
True Stories of Their Journeys into Haiti

∞

Sandra Durdle

Copyright © 2012 by Sandra Durdle.

Library of Congress Control Number:		2012923189
ISBN:	Hardcover	978-1-4797-6380-1
	Softcover	978-1-4797-6379-5
	Ebook	978-1-4797-6381-8

All rights reserved. No part of this book may be reproduced or transmitted in any form or by any means, electronic or mechanical, including photocopying, recording, or by any information storage and retrieval system, without permission in writing from the copyright owner.

This is a work of non-fiction. The names, characters, places and events mentioned in this book are all true.

This book was printed in the United States of America.

To order additional copies of this book, contact:
Xlibris Corporation
1-888-795-4274
www.Xlibris.com
Orders@Xlibris.com

Contents

Prologue 7
Eyes Wide Open 9
Santiago to Dajabón 11
The Border 12
The Arrival 18
Our First Haitian Meal 21
Life in Fort Liberte 24
Canadian Food 33
The Disco 35
A Family Portrait 37
Dear to My Heart 42
Wisly Louis 43
Jason John 45
Demostene Calixte 47
Denis Mervil 49
Milot and Citadel 51
A Day in Cap-Haïtien 56
MOJAD 63
Building the House 67
The Orphanage 71
Port-au-Prince 74
Back to Fort Liberte 86
The Bulldozer 88
Chaco's Baby 91
Diarrhea Dilemma 94
Don't Mess with the White Woman 98
Perspective 100
Farewell, Haiti 102
Epilogue 105
Index 107

PROLOGUE

I DIDN'T THINK that a one-week trip to Haiti with Alex, a boy whom I sponsored, would forever change the way I see myself and my surroundings. I didn't think it would make me realize that the material things I have in this life mean nothing at all.

I knew that there is poverty in the world, but I did not know to what extent until I visited Alex's family. Now, what was supposed to be a visit to meet friends and see an orphanage has turned into something much larger.

I now am an integral part of a village, a family, and a children's organization. I have started my own nonprofit organization for Haitian children also. This one trip to Haiti has led me to return there seven more times.

This country and these people have led me to write this book to open our eyes to the plight of Haitians.

All the events in this book are true. All the people and places are real. All the events in this book are an amalgamation of eight trips to Haiti.

The majority of the proceeds from this book will go to the MOJAD program in Haiti and help others in the village of Fort Liberte.

EYES WIDE OPEN

I SUDDENLY FELT so excited as though I had never anticipated anything so much in all my life, even the birth of our three children. All the tiredness I had been feeling for the last forty-eight hours had somehow disappeared.

It had been an incredibly long journey to get to this place, so close to the Haitian border. Just over twenty-four hours ago, Dania and I arrived in Punta Cana. We were excited to see Alex again and meet his friend Reneau, who would be taking us to his home in Higuey to spend the night until Alex arrives from work to pick us up for the 4:00 a.m. bus to Santo Domingo. Dania was nervous about meeting Reneau and spending time with a stranger although she had spoken with him on MSN. She thought maybe Reneau was a bit of a lady's man and wondered if she might be his prey. Wow, was she wrong. Reneau turned out to be a caring and responsible man of twenty-seven.

Franz is Alex's cousin who has made it to the Dominican Republic to try and make some sort of life for himself. He doesn't speak any English, but you can tell he is very intelligent, always taking notes in his little book when he learns, sees, or hears something important. I had met Franz three times before and therefore had no problem spending the time with him.

That afternoon on the beach, Franz (dressed to the nines), Dania, and I spent time with some other Haitians who worked in a small shop, trying to sell souvenirs to tourists. Alexander and Ezekiel were very friendly especially after finding out that Dania and I were on our way to their homeland to try to do some good. Franz was happy to have made these friends also since he could speak to them in their native tongue, Creole. I suppose it was enjoyable for him to be able to talk to them about Haiti and its problems.

The afternoon was almost over, and the Haitian workers were bringing in the scuba, snorkeling, and fishing boats – what a sight! The driver would yell at everyone on the beach to clear the way, and we did because he would drive full throttle right up onto the sand and flip the motor up just before the propeller would scrape the ocean floor. The boat would end up on shore ready to be unloaded!

After saying good-bye to Franz and Alex, Reneau picked us up and drove us to his home. Alex went back to work, and now we were left among strangers. Reneau's mother was staying with him at his house on a visit from Jacmel, Haiti. She was always busy taking care to ensure that Dania and I were comfortable. We had the room that Alex and Reneau share, and quite surprisingly, it was very nice with a double bed and wooden furniture. I was actually surprised how nice Reneau's little house was. It had a kitchen, a living area, two bedrooms, and a working bathroom. You could tell by the awards on the wall that Reneau was doing well for himself selling time-shares.

By no surprise at all, off went the electricity! We had to light candles all about the small house, the fan went out, and it was like a sauna in our bedroom. Without power, Reneau's mom had no stove to cook on, so she got out more candles. I can't believe she made corn mush and fried rice over *candles!*

"How did your mother possibly cook all this food over candles?" I asked Reneau.

He told me to always remember, "Haitian women know how to survive!"

After some chatting and trying to consume this foreign food, there really wasn't much to do in the dark but go to bed. We were quite sure we were not going to sleep due to the temperature in the room and were waiting for Alex to arrive around 3:00 a.m.

There was a group of men who played dominoes right outside our window. They yelled at each other and slammed the dominoes down on the table. The game was taken very seriously. Once Dania and I got accustomed to the sounds of the domino game, the power would flicker on for a while, and people would plug in their boom boxes. It seemed as if everyone tried to outdo the other with the volume controls. Although the music was loud when the power came on, at least there was some relief from the fan. Please hurry, Alex, and please hurry, 3:00 a.m.!

SANTIAGO TO DAJABÓN

D ANIA AND I couldn't help ourselves from glancing at the lady with slippers on her feet and a white towel draped over her head, sitting directly across the aisle. She had her face hidden under the towel, but we could tell she was talking on her "quite modern" cell phone a lot. When she wasn't talking, she would pull the blanket she was wearing around her body ever so tightly and stare at the picture on the cell phone. After hours of this strange behavior (and we were assuming that she was very ill), a loud cry of terror echoed through the bus. Everyone turned to look at her as she trembled and cried out some of the most horrific noises I had ever heard come from a human body. It seemed everyone else on the bus knew what was happening except us, since we didn't speak the language. Her baby had just died! He was very sick in the hospital in Haiti. She was talking with the hospital staff and rushing to make it back to Haiti before her son would pass. She was too late! Everyone else on the bus seemed to react like it was a common occurrence, but Dania and I were filled with grief and tears. The lady told the driver to stop the bus, and she, in her blanket and towel and slippers, got off. It seemed to be the middle of nowhere. I always wondered why she didn't finish the journey and go to her baby's body.

For the duration of the bus ride, people took the opportunity to use this sad moment to pull at passengers' heartstrings. They would randomly stand at the front of the bus and tell stories about the sick or wounded they had at home and make pleas for money. I was shocked when mothers brought their children to the front of the bus and used them like pawns to ask for donations, claiming that the child was terribly ill. Surprisingly, people gave money.

THE BORDER

WE WERE IN quite a solemn mood for the duration of the trip. Since we had been up for two nights in a row, we were extremely tired, but still not being able to sleep on the bus, I studied the passengers. Our bus was headed for the border, and the passengers were mostly Haitian. *They travel with the strangest items,* I thought to myself, *but I suppose they are bringing supplies back to Haiti.* Many people carried live hens and roosters on the bus. The chickens were kept in shopping bags with their heads peeping out the top. Some hung from the luggage racks overhead, and others were just tossed up on to the rack like suitcases. To our amazement, they all seemed to know the time whatever predicament they were in. At 6:00 a.m. sharp they all started to cock-a-doodle-doo. After a three-hour ride while listening to the bathroom door banging and the toilet full and reeking beside us, we finally pulled into a small town that bustled with cars, trucks, broken-down taxis, donkeys, horses, carts, bikes and scooters, and any other mode of transportation that people had seemingly built from old parts. We could tell instantly that this was the border town of Dajabón. Everywhere you looked, people were heading toward the border or away from it with their cargo. When I say cargo, I mean every random thing, dead or alive, large or small, new or old. People carried their wares, and as much as they could manage, to and from the border. Men had live goats on their heads and slung down their backs while ladies carried huge baskets of chickens on their heads.

The bus pulled in to a small dirt parking area, and before we came to come to a full stop, it was swarmed by children (some barely clothed) and men with wheelbarrows. I wondered why these men, and so many of them, have wheelbarrows. I soon found out as our luggage was taken off the bus, and they badgered with each other about who was going to tie it on their wheelbarrow. Dania and I had struggled to bring our fourteen suitcases all this way, and the old gentleman who was tying our luggage to his wheelbarrow was quite enthralled to think that he was about to make quite a profit that day.

The children in rags, called the border kids, knew every trick of their trade to ensure pesos or gourdes in their pocket. They whipped the dirt from our shoes, put flowers in our hair, and ran for bottled water for us to drink. We were swarmed by children with their hands out for money or candy. After giving out my pesos, I retrieved a bag of loose candy from my bag. What was once a group of about twenty children soon amounted to fifty people of every age.

The heat was stifling. It was like no heat I had ever experienced. The sweat poured from our bodies, and nausea was starting to settle in. There were odors coming from every direction. There were fires burning with simmering cook pots, cow dung, pig manure, human urine, and the odor of children who I'm sure hadn't bathed in quite some time.

Alex pushed us on toward the river that separates Haiti and the Dominican Republic. The Dominican side, where we were, although chaotic, seemed colorful and green. I glanced across to the Haitian side, and it was overwhelming to me how everything seemed to be in one color. *Brown!* Dry, barren dirt! Oh yes, dirt was littered in garbage. I was shocked by the amount of garbage. There was no type of disposal system, not even a barrel or bucket for garbage. It all went on the ground.

We were the last people to arrive at the border that day. This meant we did not have much time to make it across the bridge to the border. Alex tried to rush us through immigration and customs. Customs... what was that? The more you could bring into Haiti, the better. The wheelbarrows with all our suitcases were across the border before we had shown our passports. In retrospect, the wheelbarrow pushers probably knew that the border bridge was closing and wanted to get the luggage across. No problem! Just walk across the river. This was illegal, but a few Haitian gourdes were paid to security, and he didn't see a thing. Dressed in our summer dresses, trying to look our finest to meet Alex's family, we looked at each other, then at the river, then at each other again. Was this actually water? It seemed more like a flow of mud, but hundreds of people were bathing and doing laundry in it. There were pigs standing in the water; doing what, I am not sure. There were donkeys and horses lapping at the edge. There was a constant flow of polluted bubbles and a steady stream of trash floating on top. I recall thinking that it was one thing to walk across, but these people depended on this river for their very survival. Without so much as a nod from us, our purses and backpacks were already atop the heads of small boys, our shoes were kept dry by a small girl, our elbows were held, and we hiked up our skirts. Off we went, sheepishly wading through this muddy water, hoping we would not step on glass or something "unfamiliar."

From the top of a muddy embankment on the other side, members of the family stood and watched us cross. Climbing the far bank was a feat more difficult than crossing the river. It was a steep slope that glistened with super thick, somewhat shiny mud. The family members watched as we took three steps up and slid right back down into the river. I'm sure we were putting on quite a show – the prissy white girls with their makeup and dresses on, trying to climb up this muddy bank. After enough show, a few of the younger men made their way down the side to lend solid arms. Dania was able to make her way up with the help of these strong arms. I was pretty much pulled up through the mud to the top where, to my surprise, our shoes, purses, and bags were clean and lined up nicely, awaiting us.

At the top, on the Haitian side, in the town of Ouanaminthe, more family members were waiting. I could tell that everyone was dressed in their finest. Dania and I, on the other hand, looked as though we had been "dragged through the mud," as the saying goes. *Oh, wait a minute,* I thought to myself, *we were literally dragged through the mud!*

Warm hugs and kisses were the greetings we received from all the family. Everyone seemed extremely pleased that we had arrived. They were very courteous and sensitive to our every need. The girls had already linked arms with Dania and me as we headed toward a broken-down, rusted-out, windowless Daihatsu truck. This was our transport from Ouanaminthe to Fort Liberte. Where was the other transportation? There were twenty-one of us and fourteen pieces of luggage. We can't possibly – no way! Yes way! It seemed agreeable to the eighteen family members to pile into one truck, also known as a tap tap. It was an everyday occurrence – twenty-one people and fourteen pieces of luggage was the norm. People sat on the top of the cab, on the luggage, and on the sides; hung off the back; or stood on the bumper.

As we started to drive through the filthy streets of the border town of Ouanaminthe, my eyes didn't know where to turn first. There was commotion like we had never seen before, with people returning from the border with their goods. Saying that there were people, donkeys, carts, tap taps, and motorcycles everywhere cannot describe the confusion. People were whistling, yelling, singing, speaking on phones, and trying to make their way to their destinations the best way they knew how. There seemed to be no organization on the roads. People and vehicles moved in every direction, honking their horns. What were apparently roads were more like muddy pathways among pools of water. We stared at our surroundings, taking it all in, while the family stared at us. It was the first time they had ever ridden in a tap tap with two white people. Their eyes gazed at our luggage as they wondered what hid inside from the far-off land of Canada that they had only heard of.

After leaving the confusion of Ouanaminthe, the road became paved and straight. The driver turned on the Haitian music to full volume, and the wind blew through our hair in the back of the tap tap. Smiles were on everyone's face, and the joking between the family members began. There were loud episodes of laughter. We tried to understand what was being said, but not speaking Creole, we could only see who was being teased and who wasn't. I'm sure that the comments were about Dania's extreme beauty and that the young men and boys were turning cartwheels in their heads. We smiled along with them and tried to use our hands to communicate. Some of the kids knew common English words, and we were able to somehow communicate. I sensed something from these people that I had never felt or seen before. There was a camaraderie among them that doesn't exist in North America. The boys and men held on to each other's knees or sat arm in arm or with elbows over others' legs. The girls always linked their arms and fixed each other's hair. I could sense a presence of love among them all. They enjoyed one another's company. It seemed like something that was nonexistent at home. After a few days in Haiti and spending time with the people, it struck Dania and me quite clearly what was so different, why there was so much love and camaraderie, and why people weren't afraid to show affection or hug one another. Why could men hold on to one another in a tap tap and not be judged? It was quite clear! There was no competition. There was nothing to compete for. There was no materialism. Nobody owned anything, and therefore, nobody was any better than anybody else. These people had nothing! What little they did have, they shared. The same clothes appeared every day but with a different person inside. Everybody ate at the one household that had a small amount of food to cook that day. All that these people had was each other. There were no televisions, electronics, video games, books, theaters, or stores. There were people, people with nothing but each other.

and they brought out the best in each other. They knew how to pass time without something in their hands or something to watch. They made use of their hands by braiding each other's hair or playing a clapping game. This culture gave us a sense of freedom that we had never felt before. We felt as though we didn't have to keep up with life. It felt as if there was a burden lifted off Dania's shoulders since she was in no way being judged by her fashion sense, her weight, or the way her hair looked. She was just plainly accepted as Dania in pure form, as was me, as were all the people in the village. They had nothing to enjoy and love but each other.

Traveling toward Fort Liberte, I was surprised to learn that our tap tap was not even close to being filled to capacity. We passed tap taps piled fifteen feet high with people's belongings in the back. They were loaded with sacks of rice, animals, and other necessities of life piled so high in the back that the body of the truck itself hovered just above the road and covered most of the tires. People were perched on top of their belongings, sitting fifteen feet high.

Halfway to the village, we wheeled around a bend and caught up to one of the piled-high tap taps in front of us. As it turned the bend in the road, it rolled on its side, causing the people on top to go crashing into the pavement. We slammed on the brakes, and the Haitians in our truck jumped out to help. There was blood everywhere on the road where two people were crushed and not moving. Dania and I remained seated on our luggage, terrified, trying to comprehend what we had just witnessed. A United Nations vehicle arrived along with multiple other nongovernmental organizations. One officer covered the bodies of the two dead people on the ground. Eventually, our young men rejoined us, and we could hear the siren from an ambulance wailing in the distance. Were my eyes playing tricks on me? Was this decrepit vehicle an ambulance? It was missing doors! Because there were two white visitors in the back of our tap tap, the UN officers guided our vehicle around the accident scene and let us carry on with our journey while others behind had to wait in the line of backed-up traffic.

THE ARRIVAL

I COULD SEE the golden arch at the entrance of Fort Liberte that I was so familiar with from the pictures I had studied. As we drew nearer, Dania and I grew apprehensive, not knowing what to expect. The road became a track of potholes and small lakes, and any pavement was gone once again. There was a bustle of activity on the streets where it seemed people were trying to sell whatever they could to make an income. The sun was going down, and people lit candles in white buckets outside their homes and vending stalls. Chickens and roosters roamed everywhere, and there was a constant cock-a-doodle-doo.

Dogs! There were dogs everywhere. Nobody seemed to own the dogs; they just roamed the streets in search of food. People never thought twice about throwing garbage out the window of their homes or cars because they knew it would be eaten by dogs. They ran in packs like wild animals. Well, in Haiti, I suppose they are wild animals. Most were covered in ticks and fleas; some were scarred and hairless from scratching and being eaten alive by bugs. They were forever fighting over a female that would wander by or travel with the pack. After a good "mad dog" fight, the winner would get to mate with the bitch. Actually, everywhere you looked, there were dogs on top of dogs, the female usually trying to escape but losing the battle.

We pulled up in front of a concrete-block house that looked as if it would collapse if you breathed too heavily around it. The children came from everywhere. We were swarmed in a matter of seconds, everyone wanting to touch our white skin and pull our blond hair. We were poked and touched and visually explored. The children were friendly, with smiles showing white teeth from ear to ear.

Of course, the first order of business was presents, to see what treats were in our suitcases. We had individually wrapped gifts for Alex's immediate family and brought donations of clothing and candy to hand out to the others. As the suitcases began to open, chaos started to take place. I tried to hold up each piece of clothing to see who it would fit, but it would be snatched from my hand too quickly. It didn't seem to matter if it fit or not. All the suitcases were emptied in a mere few minutes. Everyone seemed extremely happy with a candy of some sort to chew on. I could feel that a bond had been between with us and the family, especially the children – the beautiful children!

After some visiting and enough heat and dust, it was time to go to our accommodations for a rest and a shower. When we went to put the empty suitcases back in the tap tap, not surprisingly, they were gone too, including one that was my daughter Michaela's precious striped bag, which she had just brought home from Ecuador. Was there any chance of finding it and getting it back? I didn't think so.

The heat, my god, the heat! Hoping for some escape from the heat, we checked into what was a housing unit for United Nations officers from all over the world. The parking lot outside was full of various types of UN vehicles, and I wondered what role they were playing in Fort Liberte. Our room was a very small concrete one. There was a bathroom with a curtain for a door, a shower stall that had no curtain and one pipe protruding from the wall, and one tap that ran water. Sometimes the water was cold, and other times warm, depending on the time of day, because it was heated by the sun in a tank on the roof. When the tank was empty, that was without water until the supply truck came by with a refill. As the water diminished in the tank, it slowly thickened into a muddy sludge. Showering later in the day always meant taking the chance that possibly you would be left with shampoo in your hair or a soapy body to rinse in mud. The water that ran in our tiny sink had no drainage plumbing; it just went down the drain and spewed out onto the bathroom floor. Our room had one small window and a fan. There was an air conditioner in the window, which came on at 6:00 p.m. for a quick cool-off of the rooms, but these rarely worked because the electricity was so erratic. There was a large generator in front of the building to back up the poor power supply. The only problem was, the man who ran the building never seemed to have money to buy gas for the generator – that is, if gas was available. Sometimes I would give him money to get gas just so we could run the fan for a while or cool down the room with the air conditioner. For us, our tiny room held no relief from the heat.

Sleeping at night was very difficult with trips to the shower to cool off (if there was water). The room was darker than any darkness Dania or I had ever experienced. With no power and no moonlight to show the way, we would feel our way to the bathroom, forgetting every time that there was a step up to the bathroom, then we would come crashing down again, slipping on the floor that was wet from the faulty plumbing. In the darkness, you could only hope that the water coming out of the shower was somewhat clear. In the morning, we would sit on our beds and assess the battery of bruises, bumps, and cuts from the night before. If water did not flow from the shower pipe, we would use our bottled drinking water and douse our heads and bodies, then lie back naked on our beds and hope not to receive extra bedbug bites. The beds themselves looked clean enough, but the marching ants were always nearby, crawling up and down the walls, just waiting for us to drop a sliver of food and then they would come! I didn't notice the cockroaches until the maid was changing the sheets one day and had my bed pulled out. Nothing could be done about the cockroaches because the manager didn't have cash to purchase the proper spray. After shopping around and buying a few cans of cockroach spray, I was given a free night's lodging.

If the power happened to flicker on through the night, the fan would come on and offer us a chance to fall asleep. When it went off again, we would lie on our beds in the sweltering heat and listen to the dogs. All the dogs were awake throughout the night. It was cooler for them to roam and scavenge for food. They hunted and fought all night long. Since our hotel had more food and aromas coming from it than most parts of the village, it was a particularly popular place for the dogs to gather at night. If they weren't fighting for the food in the trash, then they were fighting for a mate. Once in a while you could hear one poor dog, or perhaps a puppy, being pummeled by the others. There were heart-wrenching shrieks of terror and then silence. It was extremely hard to sleep at this point, knowing that there was a wounded or dead dog lying right below your window.

Every morning, without fail, the cocks would start to make a horrendous squeal at about 5:00 a.m. This screech was quite different from the familiar sound that the chickens make at 6:00 a.m. At six, the cocks change to cock-a-doodle-doo until they are satisfied that everyone in the village is awake. Haitians rise in the morning to the sounds of the cock and the hen. It is extraordinary how roosters have an inner clock and it keeps excellent time. It is also a relief to hear the call of these birds because you know that the night from hell is over and the sun is on the rise.

Next starts the calling of the ladies. As soon as the sun comes slightly above the horizon, the older ladies walk the streets with baskets on their heads, trying to sell their wares. Most of the baskets contain fresh eggs. Some ladies push wheelbarrows full of porridge or some sort of sloppy cereal. Children stand in doorways or at windows, waiting to pay a few gourdes for a cup or bowl of this wheelbarrow mush. The good news is, the morning has arrived!

We are still hot . . . always hot! There is no way to break the cycle of heat. There is no escape! There is no fresh water to douse in; we are living in dirt. There is dirt in the air and a layer of it constantly covering your skin because it is mixed with the layer of sweat that covers your body. When the sweat drips from your head or the tip of your nose, it is muddy sweat. There is no escaping the heat and the dirt.

OUR FIRST HAITIAN MEAL

DANIA AND I are still nauseous from the travel and the heat. The total change in our environment and the various smells around us have made us lose our appetites. Food was inconceivable at this point. It was time for our welcome dinner, and we knew a large fuss had been made and every gourde saved for the celebration dinner. With vomit up to the back of our throats, we were welcomed into the tiny concrete house. There was no air moving inside, and the extreme heat was making me feel faint. The room was full of people; some I recognized from earlier, and some were new faces. Many had come to gather around the small table in the small room in the small house to watch us eat our welcome dinner. Approximately sixty eyes glared at us from the darkness as we sat there. Our clothes were wet with sweat coming from our foreheads and dripping on the table. It was dark, and the only source of light for this special occasion was a kerosene lantern. The lantern gave off more heat for us in this unbearably hot room. I am trying not to vomit as I look at Dania. I know she doesn't want to eat either and wonder how she is coping, and I pray we get through this quickly. Pierre Zulie makes her way through the crowd with our food. I gaze at the dishes she places in front of us – *fish head*. It is a tradition to treat a guest with a fish head for dinner.

Dania and I make eye contact – we are now at the point where laughter is taking over. We both know how the other is feeling and what the other is thinking. What are we going to do now!

Pierre Zulie proceeded to spoon rice and beans onto our plates, then doused everything with a reddish sauce that contained a half-inch layer of grease on top. Everyone around the table seemed to be salivating at the sight of the food on our plates. I didn't know where to begin. How could I even place one spoonful of rice in my mouth with the twangs of nausea reaching the back of my throat. I felt extremely guilty for not wanting the food when I was quite sure many of the people in the room had not eaten all that day. Dania picked up her fork and looked busy as she pushed the food to various regions on her plate. She spread that food in every direction, making it seem as though she had eaten massive portions. We were still trying to contain our laughter over the situation we were in. I had to kick Dania repeatedly under the table to stop laughing and put the fork to her mouth. Eventually, she lifted a forkful of rice with a piece of fish to her lips. I noticed the food seemed to stay in her mouth forever. She couldn't swallow! As she made an attempt, the strangest snort and choking sound came from her throat. It was an alien sound. It was a sound that humans don't make. Dania broke out in fits of laughter now, not being able to contain it inside anymore. I was beside myself with laughter also, with the emerging of this strange noise. Being able to release the laughter we had been trying to suppress was such a relief. Everyone at the table and in the room joined in.

I decided that the best way to attempt my plate was to mix everything together, so I chopped up the fish head and mixed it in with the rice. This way, I wouldn't know what I was putting in my mouth. I managed to place a forkful into my mouth, but I couldn't stop from sorting the bits of food with my tongue before I swallowed. The fins were the hardest to eat, having to chew them extra long so I wouldn't choke as I tried to swallow, and I knew that somewhere the eyeballs were mixed in my rice. Someone once told me that if you chewed and swallowed without breathing, you wouldn't taste the food. This is exactly what I did, and it did seem to help.

With half of my plate emptied, I insisted that I was extremely full. The people around the table were more than happy to finish the leftovers as well as lick the plate clean.

Today, Dania and I are fans of the Haitian cuisine. We enjoy all the ethnic dishes prepared for us, although we do try to avoid the fish heads.

LIFE IN FORT LIBERTE

THE DAYS IN Fort Liberte were long and hot. I knew the water of the bay of Fort Liberte was just over a kilometer away, but the walk in the midday heat was just too much to bear. In the late afternoon and early evening, people would flock to the water and bathe. This was a social event for hundreds of people who gathered in groups in the salty water and chatted about the day's events or lack thereof. Life only happened on the streets. Everyone sat out on the street to pass the time. It seemed that no one had anywhere to go. Men didn't go to work because there were no jobs, and the younger men spent hours at makeshift tables, playing dominoes. This game was taken quite seriously as the young men slammed their dominoes on the table. The loser had to attach clothes pegs to his face, and at times, faces and necks were pinned so well that you could only see two eyeballs and a nose from behind the pegs. No one dared to let on that he was in any form of pain.

The children figured out how to devise games and toys from the little they had. Tires were cut in half and placed on the ground with the cut ends dug into the dirt. Children sat on the round part of the tire and bounced up and down. Old bike tires were spun down the road by young boys with sticks. It was quite a balancing act as they raced each other to see who could get their tire spinning fastest. The young men gathered in groups, seemingly happy, while they laughed and talked. I wondered how there could be so much to talk about when nothing ever really happened. The men did seem to quite enjoy each other's company in any case.

All the days consisted of the same routines for the people in Fort Liberte: everyone on the street. Some had bits of fruit or sugarcane to sell; others passed by with chickens or possibly fish they had caught. Once in a while, someone would have a large turtle or some crabs to sell. During the day, you seldom saw the women of the village. They were forever working at their household chores. The teenage girls would take the laundry to the well as a social event. The whole day was spent there while they scrubbed, gossiped, and giggled. Laundry was a fine art in Haiti, and I learned it well. There are four different cycles in the laundering process, causing the clothes (especially the whites) to come out cleaner and brighter than those washed in our machines at home. The girls would hang the clothes to dry in the sun. They would hang from trees, lines, rooftops, or fences. This was the time to relax while the sun did its job. When everything was dry, the girls would pick off the clothing piece by piece, fold it, and place each garment upon their heads. The stack of folded clothes would tower into the sky, but with a quick jerk and a bend, the girls could toss an article of clothing right on top of the pile on their head – a finely mastered art, for sure.

Ironing was another mastered art in the village. Everyone's clothes were flawlessly pressed. After the clothes were dry from the sun, Pierre Zulie would devise a table out on the street. She would use plywood and old chairs for the legs. She would then cover the wood with cloth. The girls would salvage the hottest coals available from various cooking stoves. The hot coals were placed into the bottom of the relic iron for heat. Every shirt, dress, and pair of pants was pressed to perfection. As the coals burned down in the iron, more would be added. Yes indeed, another finely mastered art.

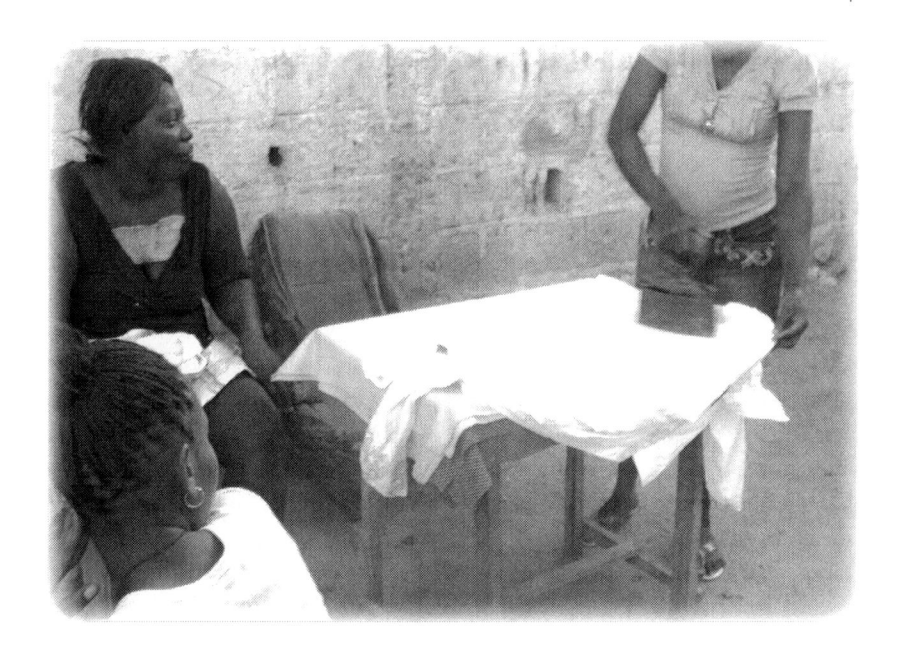

If there was food to cook, it seemed to be a full-day affair. If chicken was on the menu, someone would have to locate a chicken and then kill it. The women would pluck it and gather its feathers and fuss with the bird until they were satisfied that it was ready for the pot. It amazed me how they were able to make one chicken feed so many people. I learned that the feet were a treat, and if you happened to get them in your rice or spaghetti, you were lucky. All the bones were eaten or chewed on so that the much-needed protein would be consumed.

Rice and beans were the staple food, which was sometimes complemented with fish or chicken. If there was enough money, spaghetti noodles would be eaten in the morning, but most of the time, there was only one meal in the day at which the food portions were carefully rationed onto the plates by the cook.

All cooking was done over a charcoal stove, which was a round steel grate on three legs. The Haitian people knew how to utilize this stove as if it had a dial on the front. They could make it hotter or cooler using airflow and fanning the holes in the bottom of the grate. It was a luxury to have more than one of these charcoal stoves in a home. This meant that the rice and the chicken could be prepared at the same time.

After meals, a fifteen-year-old lad named Olrich was left with the dirty dishes. Water was lugged in wheelbarrows from the village well. The same four-step method was used for dishes as for the laundry. One of these steps included a mixture of water and a solution provided by the UN to kill bacteria and viruses.

The main gathering place in Fort Liberte is at a four-corner intersection. Here, people gather both day and night. This is where the people go to get caught up on the local gossip.

There is a barbershop located on one of the corners. There is a generator in the barbershop that supplies light and loud music through the day and night. Most of the tools in the barbershop are nonelectric. The barber uses great precision when he holds a razor blade against a comb to cut hair. These talented barbers also use a razor blade to scrape out excess hair between cornrows or braids. Shaves are also given with a thick lather and a razor blade scraped down the side of the cheek.

On the opposite side of the street from the barbershop is the cinema. It is built from sheets of tin for walls and dried palm leaves laid over tree branches for a roof. Inside are rows of broken benches on a dirt floor. Andy uses the same building for MOJAD meetings. There is an old projector that plays black-and-white movies from the past. However, recently, a DVD player has been donated, but the same movies are played over and over again each night. Pierre Zulie makes a fudge candy from peanuts and cane sugar. It is called tablet and is quite delicious. She is famous for her candy-making skills and sits outside the cinema each night to sell this delicious tablet.

Pierre Zulie, with all her faith and all her goodness, devotes her life to her family and the church. When she is not busy with the daily chores of cooking, cleaning, and laundering, she is sorting through peanuts that she has dried in the sun to make her tablet. She spends hours sorting, picking, and peeling the skins off peanuts, which she puts in her large mortar and pestle, and pounds and pounds them until they have formed a creamy peanut butter. When they are ready, Pierre Zulie lights a charcoal stove. She has to get the coals exceptionally hot to melt cane sugar into a liquid-toffee consistency. As the liquid sugar bubbles, she stirs rapidly in order not to burn the bottom, then adds warm goat's milk and the peanut butter and now uses a large wooden paddle because the mixture is so thick. When Pierre is happy with the consistency of her mixture, she dumps it out on to an old table she has devised on the street. She rolls the candy mixture out so that it reaches the edges of the table and bars of candy are cut and left to cool. The children, of course, have gathered around in hopes of a broken piece or a turn at licking the pot clean. The tablet is placed in a box, ready to take to the cinema that night, in the hope of making a profit. It seems that Dania and I are never alone; we are constantly surrounded by a group of children. If we are sitting, each of us will have a child on our lap. At the same time, a group of young girls will be running their fingers through our hair or styling it one way or another with beads and braids. Meanwhile, another group is always waiting for us to play a clapping or singing game.

In the evening when there is no electricity and it is dark, everyone gathers on the street beside the house to sing and dance by the light of a candle in a bucket. The children and teenagers alike are prolific with their chants and rhythmic clapping games. They have spent many hours enjoying one another's company, learning these skills. Without a world of television, computers, and gaming consoles, the children use their voices to sing, their hands to clap, their feet to dance, and their minds to create enthusiastic ways to fill their time.

When Dania and I do arrive with our laptops, everyone is eager to have his or her turn to experience the fascinating new world of technology. The older boys know about Facebook and spend time creating Facebook pages for themselves. Everyone wants to watch videos, especially in color. We bring a collection of videos from home, and everyone is content to sit and watch no matter what the theme. It is my belief that, somehow, everyone is taken to a different place, one that exists somewhere beyond Fort Liberte that they can only ever fantasize about.

When we are there, movie watching for the children, teenagers, friends, and family becomes a much-anticipated pastime. People will knock on our door as early as 6:00 a.m., hoping to use the laptops. The older kids love to gather in our tiny room at night when we would set the laptop on a table and squeeze on to the tiny beds and floor to settle in for a movie. During the day, I would purchase enough snacks and drinks for all to make the most of the event.

When it got to the point where there was not enough space left in the room for everyone who wanted to attend, Andy came up with a brilliant idea. He devised a screen with bamboo poles and a white sheet. Somewhere, somehow, to my surprise, Andy was able to find an old projector and hook it up to my laptop. He set the screen up at the four corners in the village and made announcements over the village loudspeaker that a movie will be shown that night for free. Everyone that wanted to attend could bring a seat or sit on the ground. Speakers were set up on either side of the screen, and with the use of a generator, an outdoor movie theater was created! Andy's movie theater was a success. As the sun went down, families came; the children came, and the teenagers came. I have since been approached to "please bring movies of Michael Jackson and Justin Bieber."

On another corner of the central intersection is what you might call a takeout food court. There are two ladies who run small street-food stands; one cooks during the day, and the other at night. Of all the businesses in Fort Liberte, I think these two ladies run the most profitable ones. During the day, the menu consists of rice and beans topped with beef or chicken stew. There is a large freezer kept by the ladies, and it contains a variety of drinks for those who can afford to purchase. The freezer does not work, since there is no electricity, but it acts as a well-insulated cooler when ice is kept in it.

As the sun starts to set, the second lady brings out three charcoal stoves and gets pots of oil bubbling. Her menu is a welcoming treat at night since hunger is starting to rumble again in our bellies. She makes a good selection of deep-fried foods, such as chicken, plantain fritters, and whole fish dipped in batter. Sometimes, if potatoes or yams are available, she makes a batch of french fries. This lady is a wonderful cook, and pikliz is her specialty. Pikliz is coleslaw made with cabbage, onions, carrots, and extremely hot peppers. Ingredients are shredded and soaked in cane vinegar, then seasoned with fresh garlic, salt, and very hot peppers. Pikliz can be eaten alone or as a salsa, but it is mainly served on top of prepared foods (especially deep-fried) as a garnish. Pikliz is absolutely delicious if you like spicy food.

Another common dish that is served on the street is chicken spaghetti. The pasta is cooked, then tossed with chicken meat, bones, and feet; tomatoes; and fresh onion. It is proper etiquette to load it with hot sauce and ketchup. Many households in Haiti serve plain spaghetti in the morning to supply their families with enough carbohydrates to get through the day.

It seems that the days, months, and years pass by in Fort Liberte, but nothing ever changes. People just seem to be trying to survive from one day to the next. Everywhere, there are ladies with buckets of water or a dozen chickens in a basket on their heads; men riding broken-down bikes through the streets, hoping someone will offer them work in exchange for a few gourdes or a bit of food; and young boys with sticks spinning bike tires down streets full of potholes while young girls on doorsteps braid the hair of a younger sister or friend. At their usual meeting places, the young men are talking and joking or playing dominoes. They are gracious and always offer salutations to people passing by. These are the people of Fort Liberte who suffer the most. These young men cannot afford to go to school and cannot work. They are strong, willing, and eager to work and make some sort of a living. They spend hours talking about what type of business they would like to own and how they would become rich. How they would be able to afford a home and have a family. There is no opportunity for these young men in Fort Liberte.

Out on the street at the four corners, whether it is night or day, there is always much for me to watch and learn, most commonly, the many ways that people use to simply survive. Although the poorest of the poor are constantly begging for money, others will utilize whatever skill they have to try and earn it. Children roam the village with machetes, scouring the shrubbery for some they can cut down and bring home to make into charcoal. Charcoal is a big business in Fort Liberte. If one is fortunate enough to have some form of transportation to travel out of the village, there is a better chance of finding wood to make charcoal. It is sold by the bucket or a large white sack full. It sits at peoples' doorsteps, waiting to be purchased.

Charcoal is referred to as "Haiti's black gold." This is because 85 percent of energy consumption in Haiti is charcoal. Charcoal is the thread that keeps the people alive; it is used to cook, bake, clean, and boil water.

In order to have some income, Chaco's mom makes charcoal. It is the responsibility of the boys in the family to roam the village and cut branches from trees with a machete. There are few trees left in Fort Liberte, but once a week, the boys manage to drag home fresh tree limbs for their mother.

Chaco's parents, whom I call Auntie and Uncle, have a small plot of land at the edge of the village; here, they have a pit in the ground where they lay all the wood that the boys have gathered. At times, objects found in garbage dumps will also be thrown in the pit. Everything is set on fire. Auntie then covers the pit with mud and leaves and lets it smolder for a week. When she returns, Auntie digs up the pit and removes the newly formed charcoal. At the house, it is dumped in a pile to be sorted by size. When she is satisfied, the charcoal pieces are put into cans and sacs and placed in front of the house for passersby to purchase.

Haitians know that the cutting down of trees and digging up of roots is causing the environment to collapse. The problem is, they have no alternative. There is very little electricity supply. It is very sporadic in urban areas and nonexistent in rural areas. The people cannot afford to purchase oil, especially with the recent rising prices.

Deforestation has led to a chain reaction of problems on the island. It has caused erosion of the soil from the mountains and deprived any remaining soil of its nutrients and made mountain crops almost impossible to grow also.

With deforestation in the countryside, people have been forced to move to urban areas. This, in turn, has created an even larger problem with the creation of more slum areas.

Old ladies ride sidesaddle on their donkeys with sacks of charcoal hanging from either side of the donkey. Older men walk the streets with wheelbarrows full of sugarcane and a machete, and for a few gourdes, you can purchase a large piece of cane for a sweet treat.

If a man is fortunate enough to have a boat, he will fish and bring his catch to the street to sell. On a good day, a fisherman may bring in some fresh crab or a turtle. Turtles make a large profit if caught, and a large one makes enough turtle soup to feed a family for days when enough other ingredients are available.

Surprisingly, there are many horses and goats killed on the roads every day. When this happens, the goat or horse can be purchased by the person who offers the most money. At another corner of the main intersection is a family that is in the business of buying roadkill and cooking it at night. The family will spend the day butchering the horse. Each part of it is used in a different manner; the flesh or meat is deep-fried in a large vat of oil, and if you can get past the flies and smell, it is yours to buy. Horse is a popular fast food in Haiti and is sold everywhere. For a few gourdes, you can buy a small brown paper bag full of hot horsemeat.

In the evening, families go down to the ocean to bathe their children before bed, and teenagers go to the beach as a meeting place. The beach is not clean; there is trash everywhere and much glass on the ground. Many drink rum there and dispose of the bottles in the water. Although it is not attractive, the beach is a gathering place, a place to socialize and get away from the dust that blows in the village. Young children play soccer there while their parents stand in the water and chat. The beach brings relief for the people of Fort Liberte, so why did the government put up a gated fence and start to charge an admission fee? Now, no one can go to the beach because if money is available, it will be spent on food, not the beach.

CANADIAN FOOD

MANY TIMES, I would watch the last of the burning embers in the stoves go to waste after the day's cooking was finished. I knew that it was not easy to buy charcoal for the family. My next thought was marshmallows. I knew the kids would love to roast marshmallows over the red-hot charcoal. And I was definitely right. The next time I returned to Haiti, I brought four large bags of marshmallows. The children were excited about this activity and eager to try. They searched for anything that would hold one on the end, but branches and coat hangers were in short supply. What started out as Dania and I and about five children, suddenly turned into about seventy. Word spread quickly about what the two Canadian girls were doing with the kids, and more importantly, it involved food. People peered out their windows and doors, and they would tell their neighbors and so forth down the road. The crowd became out of control as I tried to hand out the marshmallows one at a time, making sure that everyone got a sample. Flaming sticks waved in the air, and young boys fought over who would be next. Soon enough, the adults were in on the action. Men were eager to try the sweet, blackened treat, but women would have no part of it. As each man tried a marshmallow, everyone would stop and watch. The cheers grew louder and louder as each man ate. People were eating, and they were having fun while they did. The marshmallow roasting eventually grew into the making of Rice Krispies squares and tiger balls. Tiger balls is a campfire treat using marshmallows, cereal, peanut butter, and chocolate. When the squares were finished, the children climbed over each other to get their hands into the sticky mess. The younger children were left at the back of the pack in tears every time. This is when things usually became so crazy that one of the men would have to pick up the pot and run down the road to disperse the crowd.

Kids demanding a tiger ball.

There were always complaints of hunger. Everyone knew the words "Sandy, I am hungry," and it would break my heart every time. They knew that these words would also get them something to eat. This complaint got out of control, and my money diminished very quickly.

I was wondering how to handle this dilemma, what could I make over charcoal with the few ingredients available to me. Just then, a chicken and her row of chicks walked past, and I thought, *Eggs!* Yes, eggs are available, and so was oil to fry them in. It would take a tremendous amount of eggs to fill all the empty stomachs. *That's it!* I thought. *French toast.*

French toast has become the hottest ticket in Fort Liberte. There is an abundant supply of eggs, oil, and bread that comes in the shape of a dinner roll. The milk comes in small tin cans and must be used right away since there is no refrigeration. I am very tired of making french toast. Now, I buy the ingredients, and others do the cooking. Everyone has learned how to make it. Topped with some salt and lots of hot sauce, french toast is an easy and economical way to feed a lot of hungry people. It is referred to in the village as Canadian food. Sometimes when I telephone Haiti, my friends and family are excited to tell me, "Mom, we made the Canadian food today."

THE DISCO

FORT LIBERTE, TO my surprise, has a disco. It is set in the open air of night and has a large dance floor and a tiny bar. The selection behind the bar consists of three items: rum, beer, and torro. I have learned from experience that it is a lot cheaper to purchase the rum than to supply everyone with beer. Rum can only be purchased by the bottle, and plastic cups are supplied but not often needed. For approximately twenty American dollars, one can buy three twenty-six-ounce bottles. They are brought to the table in a basket along with a couple of bottles of torro. I sense a feeling throughout the day that everyone is waiting for me to invite them to the disco that night. Realistically, this doesn't happen very often anymore. If word gets out that I will take a selected few to the disco, eventually the table ends up with thirty or forty people, everyone having fun, but waiting to see if I will offer to purchase rum for them.

On the nights that we go to the disco, the men appear in their best attire, and there is a large fuss over hair and makeup with the girls. They exchange shoes and clothes in order to look their finest. I think to myself, *No matter where you are in the world, a girl is a girl.* All ages are welcome at the disco, and it appears that at any age a person is allowed to drink the rum without question. When we arrive, the men set out old broken tables on the dirt floor, then chairs are set around, and the night begins. The music is contemporary Haitian, and it has a Caribbean rhythm for dancing. As the evening progresses and the rum is consumed (straight from the bottle, I might add), the dancing becomes a sort of therapy. The more everyone dances, the happier they get. People will dance on the chairs and the tables. All of a sudden, these shy girls who were at the well, washing clothes by day, are on the dance floor at night, seemingly somebody else. Everyone is happy. There are wide smiles and laughter. Some of my favorite Haitian memories are of our happy nights at the disco. No one is worried at that moment about where they might acquire food for the next day. No one is worried about the ill relative left at home with a fever and no doctor or medicine. For the time being, everyone can just live in the moment and forget where they come from and where they will return later that night. For the time being, everyone is carefree, and my heart is overflowing with joy.

A FAMILY PORTRAIT

Alex

OUR FAMILY VACATIONED at the same hotel in Punta Cana for several years. There, a young man sat at a stand by the pool and handed out towels to the tourists. After short conversations with this eighteen-year-old, I began to feel very emotional about him. I found him to be mature beyond his years, but at the same time, I wanted to mother him. Eventually, he would sit with our family and tell us the most incredible stories about the life he had lived growing up in Haiti. That was it for me; my heart bled for this kid, and I told him he could call me Mom.

Alex reminded me of Michael Jackson because he never had a real childhood. Although his parents were alive, there were no means for them to make an income. At eight years old, Alex quit school and went out on the streets to beg for money. He built a box and found the necessary items needed to start a shoeshine business.

Alex's older brothers were still in school while his older sister helped with the household chores. His baby sister, Frances Rose, was not yet old enough for school. The decision to leave school was one made by Alex himself; he somehow knew that he was the one in the family that was truly intelligent.

When Alex was ten years old, the oldest of the three brothers died and left two young children for his mother to bring up. At the age of eleven, Alex's older sister, a mother of three, died in bed right beside him. Pierre Zulie, Alex's mother, was now the caregiver of ten youngsters. This made Alex somehow angry. He himself says he is "hard." I call it anger. For the next two and a half years, Alex managed to find ways to support his family. By joining the Boy Scouts in his village, he found an outlet for him to just be a kid. He attended church, went to school, and brought home money to feed the family. From time to time, in Fort Liberte, nongovernmental organizations came to volunteer among the needy. Alex liked to talk with these people, and he befriended a man who spoke Spanish and learned to speak the language. He made friends among a group of Canadians in a clinic where he volunteered his time, and in turn, they taught him English. At sixteen years old, Alex was hired by the Haitian army to perform security work. He had to patrol alone at night, carrying an AK-47. Now, the already "hard," Alex was totally fearless. He had nothing left in his heart but pure determination. At seventeen, the Chilean Army hired Alex as a translator. Now, speaking fluent Creole, French, English, and Spanish, he was able to put his knowledge to work, and not his hands, and was able to bring money home but not enough to keep his siblings and nieces and nephews in school.

On a decision that he made one night, he arose and told his mother that he was going to go to the Dominican Republic. Pierre Zulie pleaded with him not to go, but she knew that neither she nor anyone else could ever tell that stubborn young man what to do. Alex sold his moped and all his belongings, and with the cash in his pocket and the clothes on his back, Dulinx Calixte (Alex) headed for the border.

He spent months there doing odd jobs and living on the streets where he watched and he learned and watched and learned. He purchased a marionette and taught himself how to make it dance, then put on one-man shows with the puppet, and people started tossing coins into his jar. When there was enough money, he was finally able to purchase a passport with a visa in it for the Dominican Republic.

After crossing the border, he got on a bus and headed for the busy vacation spots of the DR, where he walked the hotel strips, knocking on doors, trying to find work. He went days without eating. At times, Good Samaritans would take pity on him and let him eat, rest, and wash his clothes in their homes. A Haitian man who owned a car wash befriended Alex and offered him a place to stay and a job in the car wash. This was in the town of Higuey, which had Haitian culture and a large population of Haitian people. Finally, there was some stability for Alex and some resemblance to his home in Haiti.

Eventually, one of the finest hotels in Punta Cana hired Alex as a towel boy. He traveled to and from work at dawn and dusk, seven days a week. The salary was a mere pittance, barely covering his bus costs, but what little money he had left was sent to his mother in Haiti. After nine months of handing out towels, the management noticed how Alex was able to communicate with the hotel guests. He was picking up other languages from tourists and was now speaking a lot of Italian and German. Consequently, he was offered a job on the animation team. This job consisted of game playing, fitness classes, dance classes, water aerobics, and generally making sure that clients of the hotel were happy. When someone of importance or an important group of people was to arrive, Alex would be sent to the airport as their private escort. At night, he would have to partake in the hotel festivities and get the crowd up to dance. For the next two years, Alex was living the life of luxury. It was a life where he could eat when he was hungry and drink when he was thirsty. He was provided with living accommodations and a good salary. It was a life that this young boy from Haiti had worked so very hard to achieve. The clients at the hotel would write raving reviews about Alex and leave him with generous tips. These compliments awarded to Alex led to a promotion to head of animation in an exclusive part of the hotel.

Then one day it rained. The glorious life was all to come to an end. The newly elected government of the DR wanted all Haitians out. No more Haitians were to obtain a residence card, and no more Haitians could work with a visa on their passport. All Haitians with no residence card or an expired visa were to leave the country immediately. Alex had only six weeks remaining on his visa and scrambled to get a residence card. There are many ways to get one in the DR, but most of them depend on the amount of cash you are willing to pay. Soon though, the letter arrived, and Alex's employment was terminated – he was to leave the country.

Maurice is the man in Pierre Zulie's life. Although they have never married, he is the father of her children. He is a tiny man with a large heart who always wears a smile. Maurice is a loving grandfather to all the children that Pierre Zulie has inherited. He plays with the children and holds the smaller ones on his knee.

He is a welder by trade, but he seems to be able to fix anything. He has an old bike that he rides around the village on, looking for small repair work. Maurice doesn't always get paid in cash if work is found. Sometimes he is offered a handful of rice or a piece of fruit instead. He always brings his earnings, no matter what form they take, back to the family home as a contribution.

Maurice loves hats. Dania and I always bring Maurice a special hat when we go to visit. He is always so grateful and proud to wear his new hat. Every day, without fail, he will come on his bike to visit us at the family home. We are always greeted with a huge smile, warm hug, and a toothless kiss. Maurice does not live at the family home, but I hear that he still visits there late at night when everyone is asleep.

Nerlange is the twenty-six-year-old daughter of Pierre Zulie and Maurice. She has a ten-year-old son named Nerlinx. Nerlange seems to be an angry person. She never seems to smile and is the only one in the family who hasn't made an effort to befriend Dania or me. She has been given the role of cook and housecleaner. Her days consist of work over a hot charcoal stove and cleaning up after children. An outlet for Nerlange is being able to go down to the market and purchase some necessities for the home. This is when she is able to socialize and put on her finest attire. I feel sorry for Nerlange and the dismal life she is destined to. On several occasions, I have brought her something nice to wear and asked her to accompany us to the disco. In all her bitterness, she always refuses.

Duchanse (pronounced "Doocans") is their twenty-four-year-old son and older brother to Alex. He is married and has a four-year-old daughter named Duchana.

Duchanse works for the United Nations at the border town of Ouanaminthe. He earns a respectable two hundred dollars per month, which is enough to keep him and his wife and daughter fed and sheltered.

Duchanse is very popular in the village; he belongs to various organizations that help the people. He is actively trying to get a pharmacy in the village and is also is trying to find a way for the people in the village to have proper toilet facilities.

Duchanse and Alex have never had a good relationship. For different reasons, one hates the other. Duchanse feels that he should be the head of the family since he is older. Alex is the head of the family because he is wiser. The animosity between the two continues still, and knowing how stubborn each of them is, I think it always will.

Fredly is the twenty-three-year-old brother in the family. He is carefree and always happy. He doesn't care to be involved in the feud that exists between his older brothers. Fredly has not been given the opportunity to get much education. Whenever money is available, I am pretty sure that Fredly is overlooked most of the time. He is good-hearted and would give anything to acquire some schooling or have a business of his own. He suffers from the middle child syndrome and just needs to be recognized for the special kid that he is. When you are twenty-three and there is seemingly no future in front of you, you can end up going down the wrong path. I feel that if Fredly isn't soon given his chance in life, that he will soon be headed down that wrong path.

Frances is beautiful, elegant, and smart. Frances is Alex's twenty-year-old sister. She is extremely intelligent, and Alex feels that she will be the next head of the family. She has many friends and loves to socialize. It is important to her to always look her finest, and with all her natural beauty, she walks with elegance and grace. The church is sponsoring her to get her education. She is very involved with the school and church so therefore does not have to partake in the household duties. Frances leads the life that her older sister, Nerlange, has never had, and I can feel that resentment between them.

Frances is kind and caring of others, yet at the same time, she carries a mean streak. She is not afraid to come to our room and ask for anything. I like to watch her as she rummages through our belongings and inspects each article of clothing and tests all the small bottles of makeup or sprays that lie on the table. If she wants something to eat, she will ask for it. If she wants a piece of our clothing or shoes, she will ask for it. If she needs money, she will ask for it. She is strong and not afraid to ask. Knowing this, I know that Frances is capable of achieving her goals in such a backward place.

There are five grandchildren left in the care of Pierre Zulie. The oldest is Florica, a tiny nineteen-year-old ball of fire who has a wonderful sense of humor and is always eager to participate in household chores or lend a helping hand to others. Florica is extremely outgoing and always likes to be involved in whatever activities are on the day's agenda. When I watch her, I am impressed how she is constantly happy despite her plight. To know Florica is to love her.

Fifteen-year-old Olrich is a boy who is mature beyond his years. His days are spent helping out with the household duties and looking after the younger children. His heart exudes love. Although he is not able to attend school, Olrich spends hours educating himself each day and has taught himself to speak rudimentary English. He reads anything that is possibly available to him. When Dania and I are in Haiti, we are constantly answering his endless stream of questions about the outside world and the English language.

Nine-year-old Mitziel and ten-year-old Louvence are the two youngest surviving grandchildren. Their mother died when Mitziel was one month old and now believes that Pierre Zulie is her mother. She is a happy little chatterbox who loves to sing, dance, act, cause mischief, and pull practical jokes on others. She is determined and bossy and always demands control of her surroundings. She is unaware of the world in which she lives and is also unaware that there is a better world beyond hers.

Louvence is quite the opposite of his sister Mitziel. He is quiet and always seems to have a solemn presence about him. It is as if he knows about the conditions of his living, and yet he needs someone to hold him and tell him that everything will be all right.

I don't know if Mitziel and Louvence realize that they should be in school, but they aren't. I don't know if Mitziel and Louvence realize that not eating every day is not normal. These two children, with no parents and no future, think it is normal to feel hungry.

DEAR TO MY HEART

THE HAITIAN PEOPLE have captured our hearts. Their optimism and natural spirituality are so very prevalent, and their culture exudes love and caring for one another. I find this to be something that our North American society has lost on its path through time.

There are a select few people that I have not mentioned in this book but deserve much recognition. These people have supported us in every aspect of our journeys. They were always there for protection, translation, transactions, and friendship. I could not imagine my world today without these people in it.

WISLY LOUIS

WISLY IS A twenty-four-year-old man who is trying to find a means to finish his last year of high school. He has brilliance with numbers and has grasped the English language quite well. Wisly's parents are both dead. He and his young brother, Gaylen, live with their aunt. When his parents were alive, Wisly was able to attend a good school in Cap-Haïtien. The students there were taking notes on laptops since their parents were from the more prosperous sector of the population, but Wisly, having no parents left, could not afford a laptop and started to fall behind because he was still taking notes using a pencil and paper. He could not research topics like other students since he had no Internet access. Understanding his circumstances well, Wisly asked for his tuition money back from the school. He plans on studying economics one day and considers himself somewhat of an economist now.

With the refunded tuition fees, he purchased a cooler and filled it with ice and various bottled drinks that he purchased in bulk at the border market. On the side of the road, Wisly runs a business, selling cold drinks. Eventually, he hopes to expand and sell rice and chicken also. He believes that one day he will earn enough money to purchase a laptop, finish high school, and go to university for an economics degree. Right now, Wisly has to be satisfied with the fact that he is feeding his brother and aunt most of the time. Any extra money he makes goes toward his younger brother's education.

Wisly has donated years of his time to the MOJAD program in Fort Liberte. He still plays an active role there, running games and sports for the children. Wisly has a wonderful heart. He is respectful of others and is always there, translating, giving me advice, and helping me with money. I believe he is someone who could make a large contribution to the future of Haiti if he just had the chance.

JASON JOHN

JASON IS THE most gracious gentleman that Dania and I have ever met. In the village, he is referred to as Jongul. I am the only person who calls him by his proper name because I cannot seem to make my mouth say the word *Jongul*. I believe he was given this name due to the birth defect he was born with on his mouth. Jason is not able to pronounce sentences properly although the people in the village understand him quite well. There were no funds for him to receive the medical attention he required as a baby in order to repair his deformity or help him with his speech.

Jason comes from a family of ten children with no father, therefore has had no opportunity to attend school, but plays an active role in his church. He is what some refer to as a workhorse and was extremely helpful with the heavy labor as we built Pierre Zulie's house. Jason is constantly looking out for the well-being of others. He is one of the first to greet us at the border and the last to say good-bye. Tears are never far from his eyes. When we return to Canada, I believe Jason takes it the hardest. He wears his heart on his sleeve.

My daughter (Michaela), my son (Braeden), and my husband (Ron) visited us in the village for three days one year, and it was Jason who cried upon their departure. Ever since that visit, Ron has had a soft spot in his heart for Jason.

Each time we visit Fort Liberte, Jason is our protector. Wherever we are or whatever we are doing, he is never far behind. He is the one who insists on carrying our bags, making sure we are comfortable, and makes sure that Dania and I are locked safely behind closed doors each night when we return to our room. He is intelligent and courteous.

Jason knows that he will never have the opportunity to go to school. His dream is to own a motorcycle and run his own taxi service. My dream is to possibly let him fulfill his dream one day.

DEMOSTENE CALIXTE

DEMOSTENE CALIXTE IS the black sheep of the family. He is Alex's nephew. His mother was Alex's older sister who was deathly ill and passed away one night, lying in the bed beside young Alex. When his mother died, there was much sorrow and bitterness in the family. Demostene's father was an alcoholic who lived under the bridge at the border. Demostene has paid the price for this.

Demo, as we call him, was nine years old when his mother died, and he was treated as if it was just another day. Although the family grieved for their loss, Demostene was left to grieve on his own. He was shunned because his father was a drunk, and everyone assumed that Demostene would follow down the same path. There is no support or grief counseling in Haiti, so Demo was left to heal on his own. His younger siblings were babies, and to this day, they think that Pierre Zulie is their mother.

Demostene found himself seeking something in life but didn't quite know what it was or where to find it. What he did find was trouble. At a young age, he turned to alcohol and was expelled from school. Demo was becoming very well known to the police, and Alex, who was and still is the head of the family, would beat Demostene for punishment. He put on a swagger and became popular with the young people in the village; all the girls wanted Demo as their boyfriend. In reality, it was a lonely world for Demostene.

The first time I brought Dania to Haiti was during the building of the house; Braeden also accompanied me. Demostene was the first to befriend Braeden and immediately handed him a shovel to start digging the foundation. Demo took off his shirt and tied it around Braeden's head like a turban to catch the sweat. Dania and I arrived on the scene a few minutes later. Dania glanced over to the work site and fixed her gaze on the boy digging with Braeden. He turned and gazed at her. Their eyes met and smiles were exchanged. "Who is that?" Dania wanted to know. It was love at first sight.

It is now three years later, and Dania and Demostene are still in love. He has finally found what he has been searching for. It was love. He has a heart filled with love to give. He is also a young man that needed love in his life. He has my love as a mother figure, and he has Dania's love to hold. Demostene is a changed person since the first few years of his mother's death. He no longer drinks alcohol, and he is full of self-confidence. He is kind, courageous, and is someone that his younger brother and sister can look up to as a role model.

DENIS MERVIL

IN THE VILLAGE there is talk and pride for one individual I had only heard about but not had the opportunity to meet. Having heard wonderful stories about this young man and his faith, I researched his name online and found some heartwarming stories about him. He was a childhood friend of Alex's, and they worked on the streets together. When Alex decided to go to the DR, Denis remained in Haiti to follow the path of God. He was raised by his frail mother and no father, attending church, volunteering hours of his time teaching kids to play soccer, and helping children through the Boy Scouts organization. When NGOs came to work in Fort Liberte, Denis was always first to volunteer. Having learned English and Spanish on his own, various mobile clinics would hire Denis as a translator. He became respected by many of the doctors in the clinics, and some would reward Denis with a sum of money to put toward his education.

There is an aura surrounding Denis. One always felt safe and somehow at peace in his company because he seemed to be able to communicate in a way that left you feeling warm and optimistic. He regularly prays for others, even those who have done great wrong. Denis has watched many of his siblings die. His sister was killed by the hands of others, her beaten body left at his doorstep. Still, he prays for those that killed his sister.

One of the doctors at an American clinic saw the redeeming qualities in Denis and offered to pay for his education if he were to study to become a doctor. When he finished high school, he promptly wrote the entrance exam to qualify for one of the finest universities in the DR. This school is known worldwide for its medical program, and students attend from many other countries. Without question, Denis passed the test with flying colors and was accepted into to the medical program. Although being accepted to university, he was not entitled to any of the scholarships, grants, government funding, or credits offered to all students except Haitians. Staying in the residence or some of the finer living areas around the school was not an option for a Haitian man, so he rented a small room with a cooktop, tiny fridge, bed, and bars on the windows, where he lived and still lives in the constant face of racism. The majority of the Dominican Republic's population is against Haitians prospering in their country and particularly against those trying to attain an education. The general consensus of the Dominican people at Denis's school is that no Haitian is smart enough to become a doctor of medicine.

One night as Denis lay sleeping in his bed, a gang of hooded men bashed the door down to his small room. They tied him to a chair and held a gun to his head, ransacked his room, and ripped his mattress apart, looking for his identification. These thieves stole Denis's passport, laptop with his study notes, and what little money he had left. As these cowards ran from Denis's room, they shouted, "Get out of the DR, you Haitian."

MILOT AND CITADEL

HAITI IS HOME of one of the UNESCO World Heritage sites. The fortress of Citadel sits at the end of a steep seven-mile mountain path in the small village of Milot. Milot is one of a few places in Haiti that has some prosperity because the Citadel is a tourist site that attracts foreign visitors. A day trip was planned for us to visit Milot. We rented a tap tap and driver for the day. For a small fee, some money for gas, and a lunch, the driver would take us wherever we wanted to go. When I said that a few of the family members and friends could go, I didn't exactly mean twenty-one. Yes, twenty-one of us piled into the back of the small Daihatsu pickup. Some were on the roof of the cab and some simply hanging off the back. We traveled for two hours, everybody laughing, singing, and enjoying each other's company. We brought a cooler full of water, rum, torro, and beer. Torro is an energy drink filled with vitamins and caffeine and is commonly used to mix with rum. Since coffee is so hard to come by, Dania and I always made sure that we had a good supply of torro for the morning.

Ice was another mystery. It seemed that ice was very hard to find. Of course, this makes common sense when you figure there is little or no electricity. If you were lucky, you would pass a man or woman on the side of the road with a large block of ice insulated under a thick bed of straw. For a small price, he would chisel off some chunks to replenish your cooler. Periodically along the drive, we would stop for one reason or another. When we would run out of fuel, the driver would put more in the tank from the old Coke bottles of gas that we had purchased from a vendor on the side of the road. It was only about once every half hour that the radiator would overheat, but it was all right because the driver kept a barrel of water in the back of the truck to pour on the hot radiator. Once it was cool enough to continue the journey, the fellows had to push the truck in order to jump-start it. As it sped off, they would run to catch up and hop into the back. At one point during our ride, two of the men rode on the rear bumper. When we hit a pothole in the road, the bumper fell off the truck, leaving them in the middle of the road on their behinds.

Arriving in Milot seemed somehow mystic or magical. Voodoo music was playing on the street. Ahead was the green lushness of a mountain that was so unfamiliar to us; the landscape had turned from brown to green. There was a river flowing down from the mountain and through the village. The water was crystal clear, cold, and fresh. Most of the people in our group had never seen water in this capacity. They thought that all water was brown, murky, smelly, and stagnant. Ahead, we could hear the rushing sound of waterfalls. Everyone seemed to burst with excitement when they saw the water crashing down over the cliff above. We stripped to our underwear and made our way down an embankment to the river. The water was fresh and cold; no one in our group had ever experienced anything cold before. Dania and I, being quite accustomed to cold, were entertained by the different reactions. There was screeching, screaming, and laughing as everyone tried to endure the cold water falling on top of them. There were silly games and competitions. Most of all, it was heartwarming to see the smiles and hear the laughter as they forgot about the struggles in their everyday lives.

To go up the mountain to the fortress, you could either walk or ride a horse. The horses were twenty dollars and that included a guide who was a small barefooted boy between the ages of seven and twelve. There were five girls in our group, so I rented five horses; the men would walk up. The path started out as pavement and ended up as a winding, narrow dirt trail. The farther up the mountain we rode, the steeper the trail got. The poor horses were thin and old and had made this trip hundreds of times. They wanted to veer off the trail to eat the shrubbery, or turn around and head back down the mountain. Sometimes they would just stop, and the young boys had to coax them with a whip all the way up. I bled with guilt as I rode on this poor, feeble horse, wondering how heavy I felt on his back. I thought about these small boys walking up and down this mountain once or twice a day. They were thin and had no shoes, and I am sure they were hungry as they accompanied us. On the way up, it was hard to sit up and not slide off the back of the saddle, because we were on such a steep incline. At the same sections, on the way back down, it took two boys to hold me on the horse. It was so steep I kept sliding over the head of the horse. Sometimes, I lay back on the horse as my young guide recommended while a boy on each side of me held on to my torso.

At the halfway point of the journey, we stopped at the welcome sight of a small waterfall. Everyone refreshed themselves under the water, clothes and all. The horses drank and ate greenery at the side of the path. The higher we climbed, the more tropical the landscape became. Trees were laden with bananas, avocadoes, mangoes, and limes; it was very hard to believe that we were in Haiti. Here and there, we passed through small villages where people stared as we trotted by. Ladies approached our horses, trying to sell their artwork and handmade crafts. Children ran around naked, seemingly happy. Small boys played the didgeridoo, waiting for anyone to toss a coin in their direction; their mystic sound sent shivers through my body. Riding through these small villages was like a step back in time. There was a magical air to them. I wondered if the inhabitants had ever gone down the mountain to the world below, or did they even know what country they lived in? We stopped periodically and spoke with villagers on the road, our guides acting as translators, using the English they had learned while walking with tourists up and down the mountain.

Some people in the villages seemed very apprehensive and ran to hide as we passed by. My guide explained that for some, it was the first time they had ever seen a white person. I found this extremely hard to fathom, but since then, I have traveled to the interior of the island and met other Haitians who have never encountered white people.

Cooking stoves in Haiti are small round iron grates on pedestals. There are airholes in the bottom to supply oxygen and clean out the charcoal ash. To us, this seemed like a primitive way to cook, but these mountain villages had not even advanced to the charcoal-stove method of cooking. Small fires burned in front of huts. There were pots hanging over the fires from tripods made from three pieces of bamboo or tree trunks. Chickens ran everywhere, so I assumed that the villagers had a healthy diet with eggs, chickens, and the abundant fruit growing on the trees.

At the top of the mountain awaited a spectacular sight – Citadelle Laferrière. The air was thin, and I was extremely thirsty. As I slid off my horse, nausea rose quickly in my stomach. Not realizing that my legs were numb, I fell to the ground and bruised an already-sore behind. The nausea became worse as I tried to stand up, and at that point, I learned something about myself: I could not handle the altitude. Our water supply was gone, but the others in the group didn't seem to care. They were in awe at the beauty that surrounded them and left to explore the castle and ruins while I stayed behind to lie on the grass and compose myself.

To my surprise, one of the young men who had attempted the walk up the mountain came into view. It was fifteen-year-old John. John and I had befriended each other within hours of us arriving in Haiti. He is a fine young man who has picked up a fair amount of English. He plays a large role in his church and is always helpful to others. The pastor of his church wants John to follow the path of God and become the next pastor in the village. He was exhausted and parched, but I had nothing left to offer him. He told me the others who attempted to walk up the mountain had given up and returned to the bottom. John found my companions and explored the Citadel with them. Of all the people who made the effort to climb to the top on foot, I am not surprised that it was John who succeeded.

Due to my altitude sickness, I was not able to enjoy the view from the fortress for very long. When I did, it was brilliant. You could see the green lushness of the mountain for miles around with the winding trail we had climbed throughout. It resembled a snake lying in the grass. At times, we were amid the clouds as they passed.

Citadelle Laferrière is considered by some to be the eighth wonder of the world. It is a symbol of independence for Haitians, representing the freedom of slaves and the end of the rule by France. After claiming their independence, the Citadel was commissioned by Henri Christophe, a key leader during the Haitian slave rebellion and built by the now-freed slaves to ensure security in case of an attack by France. If France were to attack again, Haitian residents were to go to Citadel for protection. It took twenty thousand workers and fifteen years (between 1805 and 1820) to build Citadel, using massive stones in hopes that the structure would last forever. It sits at 914 meters and spans an area of 10,000 square meters. The walls stand 40 meters high and are guarded by 365 canons. It has the capacity to house five thousand people and feed them for one year. Since 1982, Citadel has been protected by UNESCO as a World Heritage site.

Late in the afternoon, the guides rushed us to get back on the horses because the sun was going to set, and it would take us hours to return to the bottom of the trail. Everyone was waiting there, hungry and thirsty. I hadn't realized that this was a full-day event, and although exhausting, it was an experience that I was privileged to have. It was another world up that mountain, and somehow I would be changed forever by it.

A DAY IN CAP-HAÏTIEN

IT WAS THE last day of enrollment for school for Chaco. I could tell that he was terribly upset about something but didn't quite know how to approach the subject with me. I know that when there is a problem, it always pertains to money. Finally, after some coaxing and some translation by Alex, he came out with the question! "Could you please pay his admission fees in Cap-Haïtien so that he could return to school?"

It was only about an hour's ride to Cap-Haïtien, but we left early in the morning with arrangements for a tap tap to taxi us around for the whole day. Since the driver was charging a flat rate, I decided that we may as well fill the vehicle to capacity. I could not pick and choose who was allowed to come on this trip, so I told everyone that "if you can squeeze in, you can come."

Another aquamarine-colored Daihatsu pickup truck was again laden with bodies. Some were outside on top of the cab, and others clung to the back bumper; Pierre Zulie's cooler was filled with chunks of ice from the iceman, and I purchased bags of water to drink for the day. Once again, the guys had to push the truck so that the driver could jump-start the engine. After several tries, it started, and they dove into the back of the truck and landed on a mountain of people. Dania and I always got a good chuckle out of this while the others just went about their chitchat as if it was an everyday occurrence. In retrospect, I suppose it is.

The sun was starting to beat down on us, but its heat was not so intense with the breeze blowing as we sped down the road. This is a recipe for a very bad sunburn. It was a lesson well learned by both Dania and me. Just because you are traveling in the open air and feeling comfortable, the sun is still beating down upon your skin.

The traffic grew heavier as we approached the city. What was once a paved highway turned into another typical inner city mud road. The people on the sides of the road just went about their business as if the water and mud did not even exist. As we headed toward the inner part of the city, there was chaos everywhere; the traffic moved in all directions as people roamed through it, trying to sell their merchandise. There were horses, donkeys, goats, carts, transport trucks, and tap taps all at one intersection, each trying to maneuver a path around the other to reach their destination. Dania and I did not know where to look first.

At one intersection, we sat in a maze, and our driver got out of the truck and tried to figure a way out. There was a heated discussion with another driver about who would move first and make way. Tempers then started to flare and fists arose. During this argument, I watched men on the sidewalk as they nailed plywood boxes together. They were constructed so quickly that, for Haiti, it seemed like mass production. I inquired to Andy about what the boxes were for. He told me that they were cheap coffins made for the poorest of the poor. I asked, "Why so many, and why make them so fast?" He said that in the city, there is a constant demand for coffins and that building cheap coffins is a very big business in Haiti.

After still being taken aback by coffins being built and sold on the side of the road, I didn't realize that we had arrived at Chaco's school. I glanced at him, and his smile seemed to go from ear to ear. He was obviously excited to register, but at the same time, I think he was very proud to show us his school.

The building itself was on a backstreet in the downtown core. It was made of concrete bricks, both inside and out. There was no paint on the building nor was there even a sign. Inside consisted of about six bare concrete rooms; each had old slate chalkboards that were so well-worn that when you wrote on them, the chalk was barely visible. The students sat on old pull-down benches that were attached to one long narrow desktop. The desktop did not seem wide enough to balance a textbook or notebook, but in their day, they were probably designed only to hold a slate board. There was absolutely nothing else in the classrooms. There was no electricity for any electronic devices such as overhead projectors or computers. I was stunned. I wondered how students could possibly learn in this day and age with no technology. I felt as if I was sent back to the 1800s. This was similar to a pioneer school we might visit on a field trip for a history class.

Chaco explained that when you attend his school, the rules are very strict: Students must wear a uniform that has a badge; it has to be wrinkle-free, or you couldn't attend. You must purchase a pen, pencil, and "copybook." Lessons were taught on the board, and everything was documented in the copybook that you then used for all your studying and assignments.

We crowded back into the tap tap, and Chaco asked if we would like to see his home. A few kilometers away, the tap tap driver pulled over to the side of the road. Since Chaco's house was not accessible by road, we had to get out on a bridge that crossed a canal and walk the rest of the way. The water was a steady flow of sewage and trash; the smell, once again, burned your nostrils and the back of your throat, and once again, people were using this water to bathe, wash dishes, and do their laundry. How many times will we encounter this? Is there no clean water anywhere in the country for the basic daily chores of life?

On each side of the canal was a narrow concrete walkway no more than two feet wide. On both sides of the walkways were towering concrete walls that appeared to be some sort of high-rise housing complex. About every twelve feet in the wall, there was a wooden door with a lock on the outside. My next thought was that maybe it was an old jail of sorts.

As we walked, we hugged the wall of the building in order not to fall into the canal of sewage. The strange thing about these wooden doors was that they were all three feet above the walkway. After passing several doors, we stopped in single file, still hugging the wall, while Chaco pulled out a set of keys and unlocked his door. Everyone heaved themselves up into the tiny dark room that lay inside the wall. It reminded me of a jail cell. It was approximately eight feet by eight feet, and I knew the ceiling wasn't eight feet high since it almost skimmed the top of my head while the taller men had to remain bent over. The tiny room consisted of an old cot with a dirty blanket, a charcoal cookstove, and a candle for light. The few pieces of clothing Chaco owned hung from a piece of rope above his bed. The cookstove would only be used when he had food, and when he did have some, it was usually just rice and coffee. I hoped that when he had to light a charcoal fire, he kept the door open to release the smoke. However, judging by the smell in the room, I assumed that he didn't.

Chaco later told me that he didn't mind his hole in the wall on the putrid canal of sewage with the two-foot walkway and wooden door. He said, "Because God gave me brains, I did well in school." Being able to have the opportunity to go to school is what is important. Students from out of the area occupied most of the cells. It is very rare that a person with the means to go to school will also have the means to live in a beautiful house.

I felt quite disheartened after seeing Chaco's living quarters and asked the driver to take us to the place in Cap-Haïtien that serves the best food. After inquiring with a few pedestrians, he drove us to a restaurant a couple of blocks away. To my surprise, the building was the closest thing to normal I had seen since leaving Canada. The entrance even had a glass door, which was extremely rare for Haiti. Inside were numerous tables and chairs that were quite modern also. There were lights in the ceiling and air-conditioning. I could feel the excitement brewing in the sixteen others who accompanied us as we arranged a large table for eighteen. The restaurant was buffet style, and everyone's eyes gleamed as they gaped at the counter filled with mounds of food. I could tell that no one in our group had ever experienced a place such as this or had seen so much food in one place at one time. There was a fridge with a glass door in the corner that contained an unexpectedly large variety of drinks.

The decision-making process for everyone caused quite a commotion. People wanted to try different foods and drinks but were still somewhat reluctant. They were afraid to waste the food if they did not like it. I found it difficult to explain that if they didn't like the food they had chosen, they were entitled to go back to the buffet and get something else. I wasn't surprised to see that everyone filled their plates with the foods they were accustomed to: chicken, beans, and rice.

Because this particular day was so special and the food was endless, four of the young men stood up and thanked Jesus with a blessing. No person touched his or her food until prayers were ended, then everyone began to feast. Harmonious laughter and good cheer took over the restaurant; everyone ate until they could eat no more. When our plates were empty, Chaco went around with a napkin and collected all our leftover chicken bones and took them to the group of young, homeless boys that begged on the doorstep of the restaurant. The boys were delighted with the pile of bones as they sucked off the remaining bits of meat and crunched down the bones.

Many filled their napkins with bits and pieces of food, which were tucked into pockets or down shirts. Some left small amounts of drinks in their bottles and took them home to family members who weren't quite so fortunate. I was so proud of the people with whom I had dined that day; they were having the adventure of a lifetime and still remembered family members, so hungry, back in Fort Liberte. I was in good company.

At the edge of Cap-Haïtien stands a mountain that separates the city from the sea. I had often wondered what loomed up in the mountain and what was on the other side.

After wandering through the markets in the back alleys of the city, I had had enough. Our clothes were drenched with sweat, and a thin layer of dirt covered our exposed skin. I asked the tap tap driver if it was possible to drive over the mountain to the ocean in the hope that we might be able to swim. He was very reluctant since he knew the condition of the mountain roads. With some persuasion and a few more gourdes for his pocket, he finally agreed. Eighteen of us once again tackled our next adventure.

As we headed toward the foot of the mountain, the view was spectacular. The mountain was lush and green, which was like a breath of fresh air. The paved road soon gave way to dirt and then mud. Eventually, we ended up driving on pathways and trails, seemingly for donkeys and horses. Tiny houses of concrete and tin were located randomly up the mountain. Men, women, and children trudged up and down these pathways, carrying supplies and buckets of water on their heads. Dania and I were overcome by how hard life must be, having to trek up and down for school, supplies, church, and other aspects of life.

On sections of the road, we encountered hills so steep that we all had to get out of the truck and push. At other points, we would have to push, not because of an incline but because the mud was so thick. Every minute pushing the truck was well worth the effort because when we reached the summit, the view was breathtaking. From where we stood, Haiti was beautiful! The view to the south was of the city of Cap-Haïtien nestled at the water's edge against the green of the mountain range. To the north was the Atlantic Ocean with its deep-blue waters. For the first time in a long time, I remembered that I was actually on a Caribbean island.

For the group, looking down the north face of the mountain was like looking at another world. There were beautiful homes behind iron fences with locked gates in front. They were awestruck, never having seen houses of such size and beauty before. The thing that dumfounded me was that no one in the group had ever seen the ocean. They had never experienced the blues and greens of the Atlantic Ocean and all its brilliance, even though they lived on a small island right in the middle of it. This was extremely hard for me to fathom. Once again, I realized that they were accustomed to the small bays of water around Fort Liberte that have a dingy gray color and are usually littered with garbage.

Arriving at a small deserted strip of beach, the enthusiasm mounted to great heights, and intrigue soared. Exploration began as everyone inspected the white sand. They picked it up, and let it run through their fingers. It was not like the dirt on the beach in Fort Liberte; it was sand – clean powdery white sand. The water was warm, clear, and inviting as the gentle waves lapped the shore, unlike the murky water everyone was used to swimming in. Spirits ran high as everyone stripped down and ran in. This happy occasion made it so worth the effort it had taken to get to this place.

Seashells were another new discovery for everyone. Some of the younger children collected them to take home as keepsakes or gifts for family members. Watching the excitement of the children dive under the water and then appear with a finer specimen than the one before was almost like miners digging and striking diamonds and gold.

A lady with a basket of grapefruit and rum wandered down to the beach. She had just picked the grapefruit from her tree. This was the first time I had seen grapefruit in Haiti, and it was a tantalizing sight. I purchased all her grapefruit and enough small bottles of rum for everyone to pass around. When I peeled the first grapefruit and popped a luscious, juicy piece in my mouth, everyone squealed. No one wanted to eat the grapefruit except for Dania and I; they could not believe that we would eat something so sour. In Haiti, grapefruit is only used in recipes, or the peel may be candied when it is available. These Haitians with whom I traveled with on this particular day had never just eaten a segment of grapefruit. After some convincing, most of them warmed up to the idea and popped a section into their mouths; the older people chased it with a swig of rum. Eventually, we all sat around and enjoyed the fresh grapefruit while we gazed out at the sparkling ocean.

As if the timing was arranged by some greater power, a cruise ship came into view on the horizon. No person in our group had ever seen a ship before. The only boats they were accustomed to were the small wooden fishing boats with the tattered sails on Fort Liberte Bay. As the ship sailed closer, eyes grew wider. Everyone was full of questions. I assumed the ship was on its way to dock at the port in Haiti called Labadie, which is apparently beautiful but leased by Royal Caribbean solely for its passengers' pleasure.

I believe that seeing the ship pass by made many of the young men wonder about what lay beyond the ocean in front of us. They only know Haiti, and they didn't even know the whole of this island they were living on. One thing I did know for sure was that most of them would give anything to find out. They knew there was a better life beyond, with all the necessities and luxuries that they didn't have.

As for me, at that particular moment on the beach, eating grapefruit and drinking rum with my friends, I thought I was the luckiest person in the world. If there is a heaven for me, this was it, and contrary to popular belief, it was in Haiti!

MOJAD

EVERY YEAR AT Christmas and New Year's in Fort Liberte, a small organization called MOJAD (Movement for Young Adult Development) organizes a celebration. The group is run by Andy Jean, who is a twenty-four-year-old who is mature far beyond his years and just recently finished his high school education. This is not uncommon in Haiti since students can only attend school when there is money available. Andy is the oldest of ten children and, along with his mother, is in charge of the household. He seems to be well respected in the village, and people come to him for advice. Andy tries to give the children of MOJAD cultural development by involving them in sports and drama. When there is little else to do, he will take them out to pick up litter in the streets. Andy hopes to go to university to become a civil engineer. He is talented with his hands, always designing, drafting, or building something.

When it was time to have the annual MOJAD celebration at Christmas, it was left to Andy to build the stage in the central square of Fort Liberte. For one week, there would be a celebration every night, consisting of music, dance, and comedy. All the children of MOJAD were given the opportunity to show off their talents and show their parents what they had practiced during the year. For days, people donated wood, bamboo, nails, and hammers to the MOJAD office at the four corners in Fort Liberte. This week was the highlight of the year for the residents. Therefore, people were willing to donate or lend whatever they could salvage. The men worked for ten days, erecting a one-thousand-square-foot stage that Andy designed and engineered. It was erected in the middle of the street at the main intersection. It had stairs up to the stage that was eight feet off the ground. The floor was made of plywood and supported by bamboo poles with a railing surrounding it so that no one would fall off, intoxicated or not. Women donated sheets and tablecloths to use as backdrops; others donated carpets. The young girls, including Dania, made decorations to add to the ones purchased by MOJAD from the small amount of money they had saved. When it was finished, Andy acquired some comfortable furniture that he put at the back of the stage, arranged as a sitting area for the important guests while they waited their turn to speak to the crowd. There were colorful lights hanging from the ceiling and around the perimeter – it just sparkled! With construction-paper chains and snowflakes covered with glitter, rugs on the floor, and sheets strung all around, it looked very much like a sultan's tent. The town supplied power at night so that Andy could hire a disc jockey to run the two turntables and speakers that stood twelve feet high on each side of the stage. Microphones were set up for singing, comedy, and speeches.

Many people took this opportunity to set up tables and sell their wares, cold drinks, and street food. Others set up bars and sold alcoholic drinks. There was an exhilarating atmosphere all around brought on by the smell of food cooking, the loud Haitian music, and people's laughter and singing. You could feel the excitement among the crowd as they gathered in front of the stage for the night's festivities.

Andy was the first to speak and start off the Holiday season. He talked about MOJAD and thanked the people for their help and donations toward building the stage. Then he called Dania and me to the front of the stage and introduced us to everyone gathered there. Each night of the celebration, we were introduced in the same way and were greeted with cheers, whistles, and clapping by the people of Fort Liberte. I insisted to Andy that there was no need to do this each night, but he explained that having us sitting on the stage every night brought the people a feeling of hope. By the end of the second night, it seemed that everyone in the village knew who we were. As we walked the streets, people came out of their houses or peered from their windows just to say hello. I was stunned by this and by the fact that everyone seemed to know our names. Andy said that I was a vision of hope for the people in their difficult lives of overwhelming poverty. I felt extremely burdened. How could I single-handedly help all these people? I did feel now that it was somehow my responsibility.

The festivities of the season went on for five consecutive nights. There were speeches by the mayor, the police, and United Nations people. There were small children singing in groups and some bellowing out wonderful solos. There were dancing acts of all kinds and clowns and comedians. Everyone seemed to be having an excellent time, but you could always feel tension in the air when the police or some officer from the UN carrying a gun drove by. Andy had organized a patrol team that mingled through the crowd, making sure that a riot or fight didn't break out. He told me because of the extreme living conditions people endured, it didn't take much for a fight to break out if the speaker on stage, political or otherwise, was to say the wrong thing and ignite the crowd.

At some point in the night, the power company would shut off the electricity. A pickup truck would drive through the people and head for the big breaker switch on top of a high pole. A long piece of bamboo was used to hit the breaker, causing everything to become extremely dark and quiet. The loud music and the festive lights were suddenly gone. Only the red-hot charcoal from the food vendors' fires glowed. Every time the power company hit the breaker, tensions flared. Some nights, people would try to form a human barrier to stop the truck; other nights, they would find their own bamboo pole and try to push the breaker switch back on. When these events happened, Andy always had an entourage around us while we sat on the stage in the darkness.

It was humbling to me that these thousands of people had so much faith in me. They somehow believed that since I came from a better world, I could save them from their plight. I knew I had to make a decision about whether or not I would or even could help them.

When I think back now, I am sure that I made the decision the moment I arrived at the home of Pierre Zulie. I was awestruck when I saw the living conditions of this family. Children were sleeping on the concrete floor and using a bucket for a toilet. Even finding a glass of water to drink was an everyday struggle. The family went for days at a time without eating. There was no water in which to wash or drink. There was no sewage disposal. Everything drained between the houses on the street; the odor was nauseating and burned your nostrils. There was no electricity for cooking or light, and if there was enough money, candles would be purchased for light. All clothing was donated by churches or NGOs. If your household had enough money, the UN water truck would come and fill two barrels at your house, one for laundry etc. and the other for drinking. These people didn't even have the necessities of life.

Yes, my decision was made long before the final night on the MOJAD stage. It was then that Andy asked me if I could speak to the people. As I did, he translated, and I made a promise to go back to Canada and somehow, some way, help. That was that! It was not just the conditions of their living but the spirit of the people themselves who seemed forever optimistic. They wanted to work, and there is no work. They were grateful for what little they did have. Their smiles, laughter, and camaraderie would warm my heart. I loved these people, and I knew I always would.

BUILDING THE HOUSE

MY FIRST CONCERN was for Pierre Zulie and all the children she had inherited, most of whom were not in school. Pierre Zulie was not a well woman. She constantly suffered from respiratory problems and malnutrition and would become tired very quickly. Her son Alex was sending what money he could from the Dominican Republic. I took a part-time job near home in Ontario to start sending her whatever I could to Haiti. The money would be spent in the most economical ways possible, but when there was nothing in the house to eat, it got used up faster than we could send it.

Alex and Denis were both very wise men. They explained something to me that I could not comprehend in the beginning. They told me that sending money for food and urgent care was just a Band-Aid solution, and it would be more advantageous if the money I sent could be used to create something sustainable for the family. I understood that they needed a sustainable income, but I couldn't understand how those children could eat or even survive while I saved up enough money to start a small business for them. However, I took their advice and stopped sending money. When I had saved enough to open a small store in the front room of Pierre Zulie's house, I booked a ticket to go back and oversee the proceedings. At this point in time, the earthquake had already hit Haiti. Being in the northeast of the country, their village was fairly safe. There was very little damage done until two weeks later when two aftershocks rolled through the country and did some serious damage in Fort Liberte, which is a nine-hour drive from Port-au-Prince. At this time, work was being done at the house just prior to my arrival with the money. Pierre Zulie's sons were taking down a wall to create more space for the store in the front. As they proceeded to knock out a few bricks, more bricks fell out with them. Slowly then, the outside walls of the house began to crumble, and the tin roof fell in on the floor below. The aftershocks had loosened the bricks, and the house was no more.

The night before my flight, Alex phoned, saying that the house had fallen down. My first reaction was to laugh. The words sounded so odd – "the house had fallen down" – I thought he was joking with me. It is a phrase that you would never hear in Canada. It did not make sense to me.

The family had to split up and find different locations in which to live while their house lay flattened on the ground. The older children stayed with friends and family while Pierre Zulie and the youngest ones moved in with relatives in a small house that was already home to fifteen people. All these young children took turns sleeping outside at night on an old piece of carpet while one of the older boys stayed awake beside them for protection.

Andy and Alex worked on the drawings for a new house. Andy made a blueprint that was detailed to the last millimeter. He made a list of the supplies, carpenters, masons, and laborers that would be needed. He put a cost sheet together for me that was exact right down to the last dollar. Many of the extended family members and friends volunteered to help build if they could be fed a meal in the middle of the day. Therefore, included in the budget was the cost of food, water, and ice to sustain the workers.

The building of the house was the most primitive spectacle I had ever seen. Shovels and hammers had handles made from branches off trees. The concrete was mixed on the ground by hand. Men would mix the concrete with crushed stone that they had previously pounded down days before. This crushed rubble was part of the old house that had fallen. The children brought buckets of water in wheelbarrows from the village well, which they slowly added to the mixture of cement and rubble on the ground, under the supervision of the mixers. Other men built molds for the concrete to be poured into to make the blocks for the walls. The molds were made from any scraps of wood large enough to make ten blocks at a time. They were making two thousand cement blocks! When concrete for the blocks had to be measured, Andy built a balance scale from a long branch that was set across two pieces of wood joined to form the base. The base resembled an upside down *V*. He tied a large boulder on one end and an empty bucket on the other. When the concrete was poured into the bucket, the boulder would rise off the ground. When the branch balanced on top of the base, the men had the proper amount of concrete to fill the mold. Depending on whether the men wanted more or less concrete, the size of the boulder would be changed.

Although primitive, everything seemed to work well. Everyone knew exactly what they were doing with the materials. I often thought to myself, *I wonder if they would know what to do if they had power saws and drills placed in front of them.* Work happened in a chain. Buckets of concrete would be filled and passed down a line of boys until it reached one of the masons, who applied it to the wall. The children cleared large stones and boulders off the site, also passing them down the line till the last boy threw it on the pile. The heat was excruciating, and the sun beat down on the work site. No one ever complained about it or the fact that they were thirsty. Some worked with an empty stomach because there had been no food to go home to the night before.

While the men worked, the women prepared the one meal that was promised in the late afternoon. Rice and beans were stewed every day with either chicken or legumes. It was amazing to me how the men ate and then shared the chicken bones and feet at the end of the meal. The bones were eaten since they supplied extra protein while the feet were said to be nutritious, and you were lucky if you found one in your rice. Drinking water in Haiti comes in a small plastic bag about four inches by three inches. You bite off a corner and squeeze the water into your mouth. At times, the UN truck would drive by and hand out free bags. I would think to myself, *Shouldn't every human have the right to a source of drinking water when they feel thirsty?* Everyone ran for the water bags, thankful to be able to drink.

The house took about two weeks to build. It had a tin roof and a wooden front door. The kitchen was outside at the back because cooking over charcoal creates a lot of smoke. There were two bedrooms for approximately fifteen people. There was an eating area and a large area at the front, which would become the shop. It was a fine building as far as houses go in Fort Liberte. Pierre Zulie and all her family are there today. My heart fills with joy when I think of it.

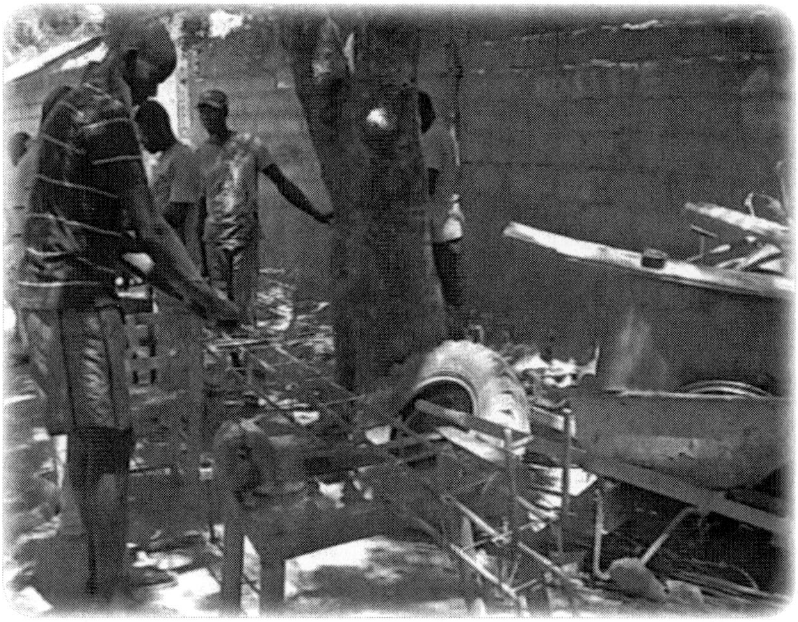

THE ORPHANAGE

ON THE EDGE of Fort Liberte, there is an orphanage. Alex is a good friend of the director, and arrangements had been made for me to spend a day there. It stands behind a concrete wall with two large steel doors at the front. It was right by the water's edge, but a garbage dumping area blocked access to the beach. The damage to the orphanage was the worst I'd seen from the aftershocks of the earthquake. All its walls were in rubble on the ground. Some parts of the roof had caved in while other parts were covered with tarps. It looked as though the concrete blocks holding up any remaining sections of the roof would crumble at any minute. The land surrounding the building, which was now basically a concrete platform, was rocky and littered with garbage. It appeared to me that there wasn't a place where kids could run or play a game of soccer without cutting their feet on a piece of glass or rock. The odor from the garbage on the other side of the wall was overwhelming.

All the activities in the orphanage took place on this slab of concrete. This is where the children ate and slept. I wondered if any sort of blankets or pillows were brought out for sleeping. There were two charcoal stoves at the back of the platform for cooking. Bowls were neatly lined up on a shelf; each child had his or her own bowl and spoon for meals.

There was no running water or electricity. Outside, there was a makeshift bathing area for the children. It was built like a box with a metal pole running through the middle. Hanging from the metal pole were two four-liter bottles, each with a rope attached. The rope was tied to a wooden pedal on the ground, and when the kids stepped on the pedal, water poured from the bottles. When they were finished washing themselves, the cap was put back on the bottle to preserve the remaining water and keep it clean.

I had prepared at home for this occasion by collecting clothes and donations. I jammed one suitcase with candy and gifts and brought a badminton set, soccer balls, and board games.

When the day came, we tied the gifts onto a motorcycle and headed to the outskirts of town. The children looked at us with the most puzzled expressions on their faces when we entered the orphanage. I am sure they had never experienced a white stranger dropping in by surprise. They were very quiet and held on to each other in fear, and I wondered if they thought I was there to take one of them home with me. When Alex carried in the parcels, their look changed from fear to wonder and perhaps a small bit of excitement.

Children were chosen from the crowd to open the parcels. They had never seen games before, but they were sure eager to learn. I handed out pixie sticks, bubble gum, and candy necklaces. Everyone who wore a candy necklace had a gleaming smile on his or her face, and even the staff was intrigued and wanted a piece of the action.

We blew up balloons, and the children ran with pinwheels. The young boys were more interested in the board games since they already knew what soccer balls were all about. They wanted me to teach them to play one of the games, and so we chose backgammon. We spent the rest of the afternoon in a great competition. The boys lined up one after another to play against me. Alex sat with us and translated so that they became familiar with the game.

These children were smart. They learned easily and quickly developed strategies for the game. I wasn't even thinking about strategy as I rolled the dice and moved my men. Many children gathered around during the games. They yelled and cheered when the dice were rolled, as though it was the most exciting event to have ever happened in their lives.

The main meal of rice and beans was being served during the time that we were there. The boy against whom I was playing and the next boy in line skipped their meals in order to continue playing the game. This told me that these kids were enjoying themselves immensely.

On a hot afternoon several days later, I took a group of children to the beach. We stopped by the orphanage to see if any of the older children would like to join us. After a select few were given permission, we had to go on a scavenger hunt to look for empty plastic water bottles. When we found an ample supply, we took them back to the orphanage. Throughout the whole time, I wasn't at all privy to why we were collecting bottles. I just did as I was asked.

The children appeared with bits of string, hair elastics, and any other bits of paraphernalia they could salvage. They strung the bottles together then attached them to their wrists. Oh, I was impressed that they had managed to make floating devices! One of the boys found enough rope to tie a large bunch of bottles together, then he tied the rope around his waist; when he swam, the bottles kept him afloat. The other children had their bottles attached to their wrists and swam with a careless freedom as if they had done this many times before.

Once again I thought about what Reneau had said: "Haitian women know how to survive." Well, Haitian children know how to survive also.

PORT-AU-PRINCE

OVER THE YEARS, my family and I have tried to get a Canadian tourist visa for Alex to come and visit us for a month or so, and each time, he was declined. On the third try, Alex was living back in Haiti after the new government in the Dominican Republic forced all Haitians out. This time, we decided that I would travel to Haiti and accompany him to the Canadian Embassy to talk with an immigration officer. This would be a short but eventful trip to Haiti, to say the least.

It had been two years and four months since the 2010 earthquake struck, and I was anxious to go to Port-au-Prince to see the reconstruction.

The bus journey from the airport in the Dominican Republic to the border of Haiti had become much more routine now, so I attempted it by myself. When I arrived at the border town of Dajabón, Alex was to meet me at the bus stop and help me get through immigration. Dusk was settling in when I arrived, and there was no Alex to be seen. I waited for an hour, but he did not show. I knew that the border would be closing soon, and I was going to have to walk across the river again and possibly in the dark. A crowd of young Haitian boys was becoming quite concerned about me as I tried to tell them about my dilemma. One of the boys had a cell phone and tried various numbers I gave to him. After an hour had passed, we finally made contact. Alex was at the border but on the Haitian side, but he had no gourdes in his pocket to pay off security to let him pass through the river to retrieve me. I made my way to the river on a motorcycle followed by an entourage of young boys carrying my luggage on their heads. We all waded through the water in the twilight as the family members waited on the other side. The boys were given pesos for their efforts, and off I went again in the back of the tap tap toward Fort Liberte.

It was eight o'clock at night when we arrived, and the plan was to leave at 3:00 a.m. in a tap tap for the city of Cap-Haïtien. There, we would find transportation to Port-au-Prince. Decisions were made on who was going to accompany me on this excursion, and I had to choose since it was at my expense. I needed a guide, security, and just plain old companionship. I had learned by now that Alex was not a pleasant person to travel with. Although I loved him like a son, we argued all the time. It took a few years for me to realize that Alex didn't take kindly to orders from anyone. When in Haiti, he has never been in a position where he wasn't in total control of his surroundings. Also, he is in control of people around him. I, on the other hand, wasn't about to let a twenty-one-year-old kid tell me what to do either. This situation created a lot of friction between us. In Haiti, when Alex says "Jump," everyone jumps. I tell him to go to hell.

I chose Chaco to be my traveling companion. Alex's sister's fiancé, Willen, was also part of our group since he knew the city well. What can I say about Chaco? Everyone loves Chaco. He was the first person I met the first time I came to Fort Liberte. He is the oldest of all the cousins and can manage a few words of English or at least enough to make some communication. Chaco is the most popular of all the cousins, I am sure he is, because of his wonderful sense of humor. He is always happy and at the same time overly gracious, always there to lend a helping hand (even with the laundry and the cooking). Chaco attends school in Cap-Haïtien. He is twenty-eight years old and in grade eleven. His greatest hope is to be a doctor one day, just like his friend Denis Mervil.

Chaco's family lives in Fort Liberte, and he is the oldest of ten children. His family lives in a one-room house with a double bed. Five people sleep on the bed, and six people sleep on the floor. This family lives in the poorest area of Fort Liberte, otherwise known as the slums. His parents have a garden and sell their harvest; his mother makes charcoal and sells it in cans. Every day Chaco's father, who is Pierre Zulie's brother, goes out to search for work, but usually, there is no work to be found. Whatever extra money they have, they invest in Chaco's education because they know that he is a very clever student.

I took a room at the now-familiar UN building but did not sleep. At 3:00 a.m. Alex and the gang knocked on the door. We each had a small suitcase, knowing that with the type of traveling ahead of us, less is better. It was a two-kilometer walk out of Fort Liberte at 3:00 a.m. to find a tap tap. The dogs were still howling at full volume. The village was asleep, but in some homes, candles flickered inside the white buckets, creating some light that helped us see in the darkness. At 4:00 a.m. a tap tap came by, and we all piled in the back. Surprisingly, the tap tap was already full of people on their way to the city of Cap-Haïtien. I dozed on Chaco's shoulder for the hour's drive in the darkness with the night breeze blowing in my face. The sun was starting to come up over the horizon as we pulled into the bus/tap tap station. The calmness of the village and the night had just turned into chaotic confusion. There were about ten buses lined up and tap taps coming and going. Each bus was an old school bus, some with windows and some without. They were painted with designs and of many colors. A lot of the buses had slogans that promised you a future with Jesus himself if you rode on those particular buses. The music blared from the tap taps in the station, each trying to solicit patrons for rides. Music and color are used as marketing tools instead of signs or advertisements. Whoever was the loudest or the most colorful filled his bus or tap tap first. Each vehicle had a driver and a "solicitor," who stood in front of the bus, offering great low rates for a ride to Port-au-Prince. Chaco and I carried the luggage and followed behind Alex. We had to squeeze our way through the crowds as Alex bartered with each ticket seller for a better price. The sun was up now, and already, the heat was causing me to sweat. Traveling with Alex was always fast-paced, taking no time out for water or food. I watched as people loaded the buses and wondered why they would have the need to travel with some of the objects they did. Our bus in particular, was more like a portable furniture store. Men hauled mattresses, tables, chairs, and mirrors onto the roof, while others tied the furniture down. I was really taken aback when I saw cages of live chickens and a live goat hauled up there also. Luggage was tied to the top and stowed in the racks over the seats. The extra luggage that didn't fit above was placed down the aisle and used as seating.

    The seating was on a first come, first served basis. Alex wanted to be sure that I was comfortable for the ten-hour drive ahead and therefore made me get on the bus and choose a seat to my liking. At this point, I was unaware that the bus wasn't leaving for two more hours. The guys stood outside and chatted while I sat on the bus. There was no air circulation, even though the windows were down. People outside were trying to sell food that they had cooked, water bags, Coke, homemade candy, sugarcane, and articles to read. Every so often, a head would appear right inside my window with somebody asking me to purchase one thing or another. At one point, a live chicken appeared on my lap, and a small boy thought I might want to buy it and take it to Port-au-Prince.

    The seats of the old school bus were obviously built for children. They were very narrow, and my knees were crunched up against the seat in front. I am sure they were meant for the behinds of three children and not three adults, and in some cases four! We sat in the very back of the bus. Willen, Chaco, and I squeezed into one seat while Alex sat next to us in the aisle, using his tiny suitcase as a seat. There was a metal bar right above Alex's head, and each time we hit a big bump, he would bang his head. He couldn't lean back because it was the back door and it wouldn't stay shut. He used his belt to configure a way to at least tie it so that he wouldn't fall out the back. He brought out a bag of cold drinks and food he had purchased outside from a vendor. *Typical Alex*, I thought, *no treats until all business is taken care of.* He is so wise and always planning ahead.

Off we went with not an inch to spare. My heart was breaking for the old lady in front of me. She was traveling with her two middle-aged daughters and gave them the luxury of the seat. She sat on one bum cheek on the corner of the seat and held on to the seat in front of her for her very life. They had a small lunch in a cardboard box. There were a few small bits of chicken, some rice, and a corn on the cob. The old woman took very little of the food, ensuring that the two daughters didn't go hungry. I thought about what Reneau had said to me so long ago: "Haitian women know how to survive."

The hours passed by, each one feeling like five. The majority of the ride from Cap-Haïtien to Port-au-Prince is through the mountains. The roads were a single lane and at some sections more like a narrow pathway. We ascended the mountains at what seemed to me a rather rapid speed. There were no straight roads; they just spiraled around and around until you reached the summit then connected to another road that would lead you down to the other side. There was no possibility for the driver to see oncoming traffic on these single-lane turns, so we always stayed to the right side of the road as much as the road would allow. At points, the road was so steep that you could hear the transmission howling under us, fighting to make the climb. I tried to avoid looking out the window since the only direction was down. There were no such things as guardrails. This may be because there was no shoulder beside the road to put them on. While traveling through the mountains, the bus driver could only rely on his horn to warn any oncoming traffic that we were approaching. The horn was taken from a train and must have been imported for this purpose since there are no trains in Haiti. I didn't realize how loud an actual train horn was until I was fifteen feet away from it for hours on end. The driver had a rope that hung in front of him just to his left. He kept his hand on the rope most of the time while steering with the right. For seven hours, we endured the blowing of the train horn as we tried to figure out some way to block our ears for some relief. Needless to say, there was no escaping it.

The landscape through the mountains was very erratic. One side of a mountain would be lush and tropical and you could see wildlife in the trees, which were laden with bananas, limes, and avocadoes. In these areas, there were small villages consisting of three or four houses. Each would always have a fire smoldering in front for cooking. The air was cool yet damp. The people of the villages knew we were about to pass through because of the train horn. They would come to the side of the road to wave as we drove through. Some had items to sell, and they would run beside the bus and make a transaction through an open window.

When we traveled on the other side of the mountain, the world outside became arid. The earth turned to dirt and dust for as far as you could see. There was no vegetation for miles. The trees had all been cut down to make charcoal, which is a necessity of life in Haiti. The soil was like powder and deprived of nutrients. This is because of the overuse of chemicals to grow crops by previous governments in Haiti. Some areas were so dry and dusty that we were actually driving through a cloud. We could not see out the window, and it had to be closed so that we could breathe. This is when it would become extremely hot on the bus. It was what I would call a lose-lose situation.

98% of Haiti has been deforested due to the reliance of charcoal production. Therefore, the landscape is reduced to powdery sand. In some areas, a chalky white powder. In heavy rainfalls, these areas are very vulnerable to floods and mudslides since there is no stability in the soil. The wind causes constant erosion in these areas, creating large crevices in hills and mountains. These crevices produce peaks that hang loosely, waiting for the forces of Mother Nature to cause destruction.

After about seven hours of riding, the passengers were starting to become very irritable. Many, including me, had nature calling. It was approximately three in the afternoon, and it was becoming hard to hold in, especially when we traveled on such bumpy roads. I realized then that I had not used the facilities since 3:00 a.m., which was twelve hours earlier. The guys had been able to relieve themselves at the station before they got on the bus. The driver would not stop the bus for the passengers. People were getting angry, yelling in Creole, "Chauffer – stop the bus, we have to pee!" He drove on. Alex stood up and unzipped his jeans. Everyone glared at him as he pulled his jeans halfway down his legs and stood in his underwear. He then bellowed at the driver and said, "If you don't stop the bus for the people to pee, I will pee right here!" The bus stopped.

We stopped in an area that was beautiful and green. You could hear buzzing in the jungle by the side of the road. Everyone made their way off the bus through the front door or the back, whichever was easiest. Many people had to climb over suitcases and whatever other objects were obstructing the aisle. People were elated to be off the bus and relieve themselves. When we stopped, villagers from the surrounding houses came out to watch the commotion. I assumed that people would go into the brush or jungle to pee, but I was wrong. Ninety people had no problem just dropping their pants to pee on the side of the road – men and women, young and old, number one or number two. There was no embarrassment; they simply had to use the facilities, and the facilities happened to be the side of the road. Except for me, the white girl! What would the white girl do? Actually, I didn't know what to do. I stood there in amazement as I pondered whether or not to squat and pee. I could feel their eyes upon me, some saying, "Aren't you going to go, lady?" and others saying, "I wonder what the white woman is going to do." I asked Alex if I could go into the bush, but the driver was already telling us to get back on the bus. Alex asked, "Why do you have to go into the bush? If you have to pee, just pee!" I got back on the bus.

After riding through the mountains all day, it was a great relief to be on the highway that led to the capital city. The highway ran beside the ocean, which was a refreshing sight. I had a hard time with the correlation of the ocean and Haiti at this time. I had never actually seen the ocean and its brilliant colors while traveling in Haiti. I was accustomed only to the lifeless gray waters of Fort Liberte Bay. Here at the ocean's edge, there were extravagant houses with large yachts parked in front. The beach areas had white powdery sand like I had seen on other islands but didn't think existed in Haiti. Most of the homes and yachts flew American flags. I was told that many people come over by boat from Miami because there is a large population of Haitians in Miami, and those who can afford it have a house in both countries.

As we turned off the main highway, the view became the Haiti with which I was familiar. Roads were once again filled with potholes, and most of them were filled with water and mud. I sensed we were approaching the outer limits of Port-au-Prince by the amount of traffic heading in our direction. Willen told me to look out my window into the distance, at a faraway hill. It seemed to be spotted with white dots. I assumed they were grazing sheep, but as we drew near, my heart began to sink into the pit of my stomach. This was the first actual sighting of the effects of the earthquake – the white dots were tents. Thousands of tents perched on a hillside, filled with displaced people. I had seen the images on television many times, and I was now seeing the real thing. The pictures on TV did not give the full impact of this horrific sight.

The bus stopped, and to my surprise, it was just the four of us who got off. Willen had arranged for us to be picked up by four mototaxis. From here, we would be traveling to his sister's home to eat and visit before finding accommodations for the night. Each of us was on the back of a motorcycle with our suitcase on the driver's lap. The paved roads turned into dirt roads. Traveling on these dirt roads was an adventure. For the most part, they were nonexistent since they had been washed out by rain, and there was no place for drainage because concrete houses lined the sides of the road. What had been potholes of water when we started were now small ponds. Eventually, the road became a river. We drove right on through, and the water was up to my knees. It sprayed up from the sides of the tires in the form of mud, and we were all drenched and had splatters of mud on our faces, arms, and hair. After passing the tent city and not being able to shake my feeling of gloominess, this was well-needed comic relief. As we rode, I started to laugh. My laughter became uncontrollable as I saw the others getting soaked. Still having not yet been able to use the facilities, I was having a hard time to control the contents of my bladder. Need I say more!

The home of Willen's sister was down a narrow concrete alleyway that had houses on both sides. She lived up a long flight of stairs at the back of one. She actually lived on the roof of one of these houses in a makeshift two-room house that Willen had built for her. The remaining part of the roof was open to air and partially covered with a blue tarp, underneath which she cooked and did laundry. There was no barricade around the edge of the roof, nor was there any type of railing as you ascended and descended the narrow concrete staircase. No one seemed to mind as five young children played atop the roof and ran up and down the stairs. I couldn't take my eyes off them, knowing that one fall off the roof onto the concrete alley below would cause death.

Willen's sister and children were delightful. She was very hospitable, bringing us buckets of water and soap for bathing. The house was prepared for our arrival. One room was used as dining room and the other as a sleeping room as is typical of most Haitian homes. The table was set for four with all its fine décor. It was a beautiful wooden dining set that had been left by their mother from better days of the past. In all my time in Haiti, I had never seen a feast such as the one she had prepared for us. There was a salad made with fresh vegetables. This was quite surprising to me since I had never seen these in Fort Liberte. Willen explained that being in Port-au-Prince, one had access to a lot more variety in many things. We were served fried chicken and fish. There was rice and beans, macaroni and cheese, carrots, salad, and freshly squeezed mango juice. I wondered how she could have afforded to purchase all this food and had to assume that Willen, being a well-respected mason and carpenter, probably made more money than the average person and had covered the expenses.

Everyone was in good spirits. We were happy to be clean, happy to be full, and most of all, happy to be off the bus! Chaco in particular was already having the time of his life. He was absorbing every aspect of our journey since this was his first adventure away from the Fort Liberte, Cap-Haïtien area, known as the Northeast. Chaco's eyes popped from their sockets when he saw the spread of food on the table. It was the first time he had ever sat down to a table and eaten until his stomach was content and then eaten some more. He was quite used to eating a small amount once a day or not eating at all. For her family, Chaco's mother makes a drink over the fire that consists of corn, rice, and beans. In this form, the food stretches further instead of being eaten it in its regular state from a bowl or plate.

Willen had arranged to borrow a truck from a friend, providing I paid for the gas. It was dark, and we still had to venture into the depths of the city to find a place to sleep. The traffic in downtown Port-au-Prince was bedlam. Music blared from tap taps, and people constantly banged on their horns, trying to pass each other or telling one another to speed up or move. At times, drivers would find themselves in situations where no one could move since they had each other blocked in all directions. Some drivers would get out of their cars and try to systematically figure a way to move on. Other times, drivers would all get out of their vehicles, yelling at each other, blaming and cursing each other for the predicament they were in. It took an hour to move a kilometer at certain times of the day. Fights between drivers would break out, and Alex would insist we put the windows up in our truck. At one point, two drivers were fighting as we sat waiting to move ahead, and Alex had to get out of the truck and break them up. I asked him why this happened so much. He told me that the tensions are high in the city, and that it was really just a big part of the Haitian culture.

We had to be at the Canadian Embassy at 7:00 a.m. the next morning. We stopped at several hotels, looking for a room, but the prices were astronomical at one hundred US dollars per night. We needed two rooms at least, and at these prices for one concrete square with a tiny bed, Alex refused all of them. I agreed with Alex, but I was getting to the point where I would sleep anywhere for any price since the last time I had slept was in Canada. It didn't dawn on me until then that I hadn't slept for the better part of three days.

In a somewhat nicer are of the city, called Delmas, we passed a sign that said, "Lodge ahead." When we found it, it was extremely modern looking and clean. We went in and spoke to the owner who was Haitian American and spoke English, and I was glad to be able to understand the negotiations between him and Alex. It was good to speak to someone about Canada and the United States since I had not been involved in an elongated conversation with anyone for days. Although Alex speaks English, he is not one for conversation when traveling. This lodge turned out to be the perfect solution for us. It was opened as a place for members of NGOs to live while they were in Haiti. The rooms consisted of six sets of bunk beds. There was a fan by every bed and air-conditioning in each room. The bathrooms were clean and had all the amenities. There were sitting areas among tropical garden settings, an indoor lounge area, and a fully equipped kitchen that provided free coffee at any time of the day. You could cook or have a maid cook for you. Everything was spotless. The owner said that he wanted to open a place where people from NGOs from all over the world could come and stay with all the comforts of home. A place where they could eat the food they were accustomed to and to relax and mingle after a hard day of work. For one hundred US dollars a night, you could have a bed and use the facilities in the lodge. There were rooms for women and rooms for men. This concept did not go over well with Alex and Willen. They didn't want to sleep in a room full of strange men, so they opted to go back and sleep at Willen's sister's house. Chaco, on the other hand, was wide-eyed again. He was already enjoying a free cup of coffee and relaxing on the big couch in the lobby. I don't think he wanted to go anywhere. He had no problem sleeping in a bed to himself, strangers or no strangers.

The next morning, Alex and Willen arrived at 9:30 a.m., and we were two and a half hours late already. The traffic had held them up for three hours. While we waited for Alex and Willen to arrive, Chaco and I explored the lodge. Everything about it was new and exciting for him. We went to the kitchen, and I explained about the fridge. He couldn't grasp the concept that people would buy a large amount of food and that the fridge would keep it cold. Chaco had only ever purchased small amounts of rice and beans at a time and maybe a chicken or some fish to accompany if the funds were available. The freezer was another concept that baffled him. Why would people spend money to buy food and then freeze it? I was enjoying myself trying to explain these things to Chaco. He made me laugh with his reactions.

Next, I took Chaco to the laundry room. When I thought the fridge and stove had boggled his mind, it was nothing compared to the electric washer and dryer. We gathered all our dirty clothes from our rooms, and I told him to put them in the washer then showed him the soap. All he had to do was push the button and the clothes would wash themselves? He watched as the gyrator churned back and forth, somewhat concerned about whether his clothes would come out in one piece. After the wash load, he filled the dryer, and I showed him how to put in a fabric-softener sheet. Push another button and the clothes would dry? Hard to believe! When the buzzer sounded, Chaco ran to the dryer to inspect. *Blown away* is the term I can best use to describe his reaction.

Of the whole experience of staying at the lodge, I think Chaco liked the shower most of all. Every spare moment for Chaco was spent in the shower. At one point, he was in the shower so long that the other men in his room were getting frustrated that they couldn't get time for their shower. Chaco then asked me if he could use the women's shower. I consulted the ladies, and they didn't seem to mind. After using the ladies shower four times in one day, the ladies told me that maybe it would be better if Chaco went back to using the men's shower.

I think these events with Chaco and the electric appliances are one of my fondest memories, and I shall treasure them forever.

The first five hours spent at the embassy were only the first of three trips we had to make there. When we finished there, Willen took us on a tour of Port-au-Prince. The city consisted of some fairly nice sections while others, I'm sure, were some of the most devastated places on earth. The largest tent cities that housed displaced people from the earthquake were the outside of the city. People had randomly put up tents or built shelters from anything available. The sidewalks were lined with tiny square shelters made from tin, pieces of wood, fabric, signs, and cardboard. There were mothers in these shelters, tending to children, most of them with a baby in one arm. Fires of charcoal or whatever garbage was available burned on the sidewalk for cooking. Inside the shelters (or at least the ones I could see into), people slept on dirty pieces of cardboard, the bare ground, or maybe a piece of cloth. Many children have protruding bellies, which was evidence of malnutrition, and many have herniated belly buttons. These shelters were so unstable that the slightest wind or rainfall would send a family right back to where they had started. People were just trying to survive. They asked and they begged for the slightest donations that anyone could give. The vehicles of NGOs from around the world were everywhere on the streets. At times, there were more NGO vehicles and UN trucks than local Haitian traffic. Most of the vehicles seemed to be there for security. They surveyed and patrolled. Where were the people from these organizations who were there to distribute food or give medical attention to the people?

We ventured on through the city to where the government buildings stood. You could tell that prior to the tents, shelters, and large piles of rubble, this area had been extremely beautiful. The park surrounding the buildings was now a rather large tent city. The grass in front of the government buildings was still green, so very green that it looked oddly out of place in this demolished landscape with its toppled statues and monuments. Across the grass in the distance lay the white home of the Haitian government leader. These buildings caught me off guard with the enormity of their size. The presidential palace was exquisite with its white exterior against the blue sky and green grass. The walls of the palace were still standing, but the roof, which consisted of three domes, had collapsed. It seemed to be resting on the walls in a heap of rubble. It was as though, at any moment, the walls would collapse from the weight of the roof. Over two years had passed since the earthquake, and it appeared that the ruins still sat in the same condition as they did the day the quake struck. People were still gathered at the fence that surrounded the grounds, peering at the fallen palace with disbelief in their hearts. Looking at the palace in this condition could not possibly give the people hope for the future.

Next, Willen took us to see the most disturbing place of all. It was another tent city that consisted of tens of thousands of tents. The city was situated on a sea of mud. Rainwater was lying in the main areas, creating massive mud puddles around the tents. Women used this water for washing their clothes and bathing their children. People went about their daily routines in the mud as though it was the norm. Children kicked a deflated soccer ball to one another on an open piece of land that had turned into a swamp. The odors were deplorable. Alex forbade me to get out of the truck and venture into the tent city for fear of my safety. I suppose he was right, but I insisted that he let me at least go to the entrance area where women were gathered as they cooked over fires. I felt an overwhelming need to hug these women and give them a few gourdes. When Alex was preoccupied in the front seat, I opened my door and jumped out of the truck. I spoke to the ladies with using few words or Creole I had in my vocabulary. They seemed mesmerized as I approached with open arms, and I went into my purse instantly and offered Chiclets to all. A bond was made. I asked the ladies to show me what they were cooking, and they were very responsive. I was shocked to see that there was no actual food in the pots. The ladies were cooking mud, making something that was in no short supply – *mud!*

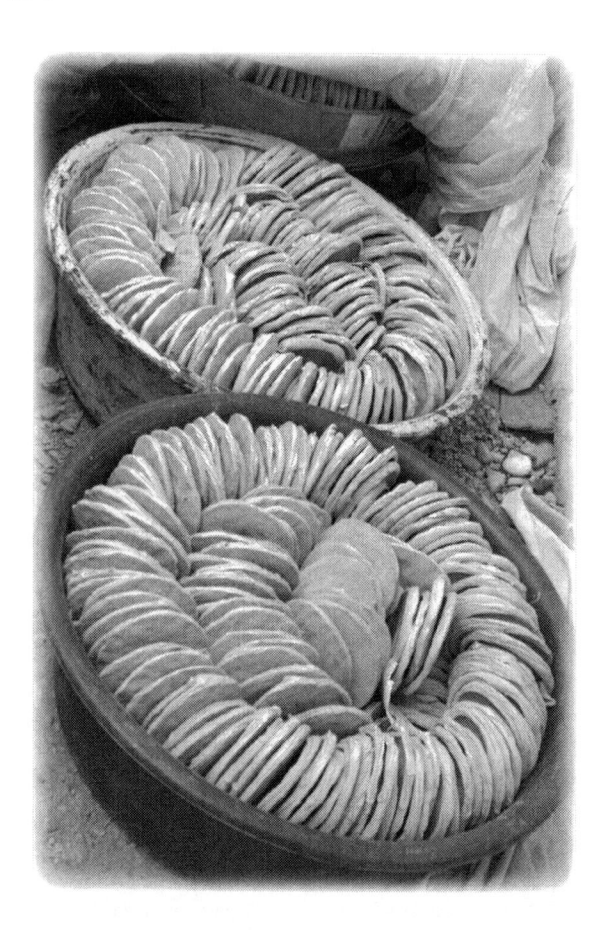

    Haitian women make mud cakes to fill the stomach when there is nothing else to eat. They are eaten only to take away the hunger pangs; they have no nutrient factor. In an area as impoverished as the tent city, mud cakes are also made to sell. Mud cakes are made with water, salt, margarine, and dirt. When the mixture is at the proper consistency, the mixture can be cut or molded into various shapes. The cakes or cookies are then baked in a charcoal oven or in the sun.

Sitting in the evening traffic on the way back to the lodge, I didn't speak with the others. I knew what we had witnessed today was not causing them any distress. I could feel the tears welling up in my eyes, and if I spoke aloud about my sorrow at that moment, I knew that Alex would reply, "Never mind, Mom, that is the Haitian life."

I would then think to myself, *Don't you care, Alex, these are your fellow countrymen?* How could he care? He is struggling in his own life, trying to provide food, shelter, and education when he can. His own family goes hungry. He cannot add more stress on himself by worrying about others.

Gazing out the window, I pondered and watched the people on the streets. Everyone was just trying to survive. It was not like the streets at home where people were walking just for the sheer pleasure of it, hand in hand, smiles on faces, or perhaps just walking the dog. These streets were where people tried to survive day by day, hour by hour. There were ill people that just lay in one spot as others stepped over them. There were numerous people without limbs. There were blind people and many small naked children seemingly without parents or a home. *Are we still on planet Earth, or did planet Earth suddenly come to an end and this is what remains? Is this just a bad dream and I will wake up? Are we human beings allowing our fellow man to live in these conditions?*

It takes four hours to fly to Haiti from Toronto, I thought. *It takes one hour and a half to fly from Miami. Haiti is a few hours away from two of the richest countries in the world, yet it has been forgotten. How do we let our neighbors exist without the basic human necessities of life? A human being should have the right to a clean drink of water or a place to go to the bathroom. A person should not have to eat mud to survive while we at home think nothing of eating at a restaurant and spending two hundred dollars on one meal. How do we justify rewarding ourselves with the things in life that we don't really need but feel we deserve?* These thoughts crowded my mind. Suddenly I felt ashamed of what I had and where I came from. Anger was my next emotion. *These are people*, I thought to myself. *How can I help? How can I at least make a difference in the smallest way?* All these questions would be answered in time, but for now, I was physically and mentally exhausted from what I had seen this day.

BACK TO FORT LIBERTE

BY THE THIRD day in Port-au-Prince, I was ready to go home. I realized then that I had referred to Fort Liberte as home. After travelling there so often with Dania, in some strange way, it felt like our second home. On the fourth morning, Alex flagged down a tap tap that took us to the bus station in Port-au-Prince. Not surprisingly, it was much like the one in Cap-Haïtien but twice as crowded and just as confusing. We trekked through mud while Alex bartered for the cheapest ride back to Cap-Haïtien. I promised myself that I would not fall for the same trick again and be put on the bus two hours before departure.

Well, I did! Alex promised me that the bus was about to leave at any time, and I should get on to save myself a comfortable seat. I believed him at the time, but in retrospect, I wondered if he just didn't want to look after me in all the crowds and confusion.

The bus was just as full as on the trip south. It was hot, it was sticky, and it was loud. People seemed to be more exuberant on this bus. They yelled back and forth at each other. Some laughed, some sang, and some listened to music. This went on for most of the ride. At the same time through all the commotion, the driver would pick up people who had goods to sell. The salesman would stand at the front of the bus and try to yell louder than everyone else as he pitched his wares. Some were selling candies they had made while others tried to sell you their magic tonics – one bottle and all your problems would be solved, another bottle and all your ailments would disappear. Street food vendors jumped aboard. As I was hungry, these were the salesmen that caught my attention. Most of them sold the same thing: a cone-shaped, rolled brown paper containing deep-fried pieces of pork and plantain fritters. They were topped with pikliz and a white hollandaise type of sauce. Delicious!

This time, travelling in the opposite direction, I was better able to observe what I had missed on the trip to the capitol. The land formations that stood out for me the most were the dry sand cliffs. These were large sections in the sides of hills and mountains where huge pieces of the earth had just fallen off. The cliffs looked very fragile. At places you could see where the wind had eroded the dry earth right out of the side of a mountain, creating large crevices where you could swear that the top of the crevice would fall off at any moment. Rain, I knew, was very hazardous for these areas, and now I could see why. *Driving through these dry areas,* I thought to myself, *it must be just like driving through a snowy mountain range, waiting for an avalanche to happen.*

Since we were travelling mainly downhill this time, the transmission didn't have to work as hard. I could tell this by the speed at which we were moving. At times, we put our heads in our hands on the seat in front of us and said a prayer to God that the bus driver knew what he was doing. We travelled around and around as we descended. At points when you thought you were already going much too fast, the driver would speed up, and on this trip, the driver didn't pull on his train-horn cord; he had it tied down so that it blew a constant bellow.

At one point, the man in front of me turned around and said to me in fear, "Holy shit, we are going to die!"

"You speak English!" was my response. Peter was a Haitian American who had been a United States Marine and was travelling back from Port-au-Prince after looking at the possibility of opening a nightclub there; he had not been back to Haiti in over twenty years. As a marine, he had done tours of duty in Bosnia and Iraq and survived the most dangerous of situations but was paranoid on this bus ride through the mountain range. From that point on, Peter and I became friends. I constantly teased him about being the US Marine who was terrified of a little bus ride through Haiti.

THE BULLDOZER

THE BUS CAME to a stop, seemingly for no reason, in the middle of the road. We waited for some sort of explanation as to why we sat for so long. Being at the back of the bus, we hadn't realized that a portion of the road ahead had caved in, forming a deep crevice that was much too large to drive over. The driver told us all to get off the bus while he pulled it over to make room for a bulldozer that was on its way to repair the road. Everyone sat perched along the sides of the road and waited, and waited, and waited some more.

The bulldozer was a Caterpillar and a very large one at that. It arrived on the back of a flatbed truck. The width of the flatbed was a much wider than the width of the road, therefore, in order for it not to fall off the edge of the cliff on one side, the driver had to park as close to the embankment on the opposite side of the road as he could. The inner side of the road had a ditch with water and mud in it from a small flow coming down the mountain. As the driver slowly crept toward us, he stayed very tight to the edge of this ditch. People were gesturing with their hands, and the male passengers yelled at the driver to turn this way and or that until they were satisfied that the flatbed was positioned correctly.

Slowly, the tires nearest the ditch started to sink, while the tires on the cliff side of the road were on dry, hard ground. The flatbed was starting to tip on an angle, so it had to be unhitched from the truck. The dozer, still sitting on the flatbed, was now on an angle as the driver started it up. The tires were sinking quickly as the men once again voiced their opinions about how the bulldozer should be driven off the flatbed in order not to tip over. The driver seemed overwhelmed and, I am sure, quite embarrassed as voices rose and arms flailed. He started to back the bulldozer off, turning it at the same time to keep extra weight from the sinking tires underneath, but he turned the dozer too far and left himself with no possibility of backing off. He pulled forward to straighten out a little, and as he did, the flatbed tilted to about a forty-five-degree angle. The inside tires were now completely sunk in the mud while the tires on the outside were firmly on the road.

I started to feel compassion for the young man driving the bulldozer. Some of the men from the bus were terribly angry with him while others laughed. I told my new friend Peter that it was time for a United States Marine to take charge. The young driver made one more try at backing off the flatbed and one more having to pull forward. We all knew what was going to happen, and it did. The large Caterpillar tipped on its side and landed in the ditch along with the driver. *This could only happen in Haiti*, I thought. I could not ever imagine a bulldozer falling off a flatbed in Canada.

A couple of the men pulled the driver out of the bulldozer. Now that the weight was no longer on the flatbed, the tires still on the road started to rise up, causing the flatbed to sit at an even steeper angle. This turned out to be a godsend in the sense that the driver would now have to bring the truck to the back of the flatbed and pull the bulldozer from the ravine. Enough room was now available as he backed the truck up and carefully turned it around. The men hooked a large winch to the dozer, and the truck driver slowly pulled forward. As he did, the dozer made its way up on to the road. Everyone cheered and clapped. The poor driver was able to muster a small smile, feeling somewhat better about things.

The next step was to get the sunken flatbed that was perched on a seventy-degree angle out of the ditch. The men once again hooked up the winch; other men hooked a heavy chain from the bulldozer to the flatbed. Peter hopped in the dozer and the driver into his truck. They slowly drove forward, and to everyone's surprise and relief, the flatbed emerged from the ravine of mud.

The driver proceeded to the task at hand, which was to repair the road ahead. By this time, hours had passed, and I had forgotten all about the hole in the road.

When it was safe enough, the bus driver drove the bus across the hole and then told us to get back aboard. Since our foursome was sitting at the very back, we decided to enter through the back door instead of climbing over all the articles that blocked the aisle. Everyone boarded, and we tried to get someone to open the back door from within. Just then the bus left. The four of us ran behind, trying to keep up to the bus. I was hot, thirsty, and tired; there was no way I could go on as the bus disappeared from sight. Alex told me to stay put with Willen, and he and Chaco kept running to stop the bus. At some point, almost a kilometer down the road, someone realized that we were not present, and Peter got the driver to stop the bus. Chaco ran ahead to the bus while Alex ran back to get Willen and me.

I had been forewarned about bus trips through Haiti, going to and from Port-au-Prince. I had been told to leave extra travelling time since the busses usually have mechanical failures. I never dreamed that our delay would be due to the spectacle of a bulldozer and a flatbed on their sides in a deep, muddy ditch by the edge of a cliff. *Only in Haiti*, I thought again. It was getting to the point where nothing would surprise me anymore.

CHACO'S BABY

UPON ARRIVAL BACK in Fort Liberte, we were elated to be home. Friends and family gathered to greet us and hear the tales about Port-au-Prince. It was already late, but sitting out in front of Pierre Zulie's house by the light of candles in white buckets, it felt like home. This is when Chaco received word that his baby had been coughing and was very lethargic. His son was born on June 23, 2012, which is the same day as my oldest daughter's birth. Although Chaco is still struggling financially to remain in school, he is a good and loving father to his baby boy, and the mother, Natasha, is eighteen years old and extremely mature. Natasha's parents died some time ago, so she was already looking after her ten-year-old brother and twelve-year-old sister and now had to leave school in order to care for her own baby. The three siblings live with their grandmother, who is not a healthy woman. There is no source of income for the household. Therefore, the addition of a newborn creates a dire situation for her family.

During Natasha's pregnancy, Chaco phoned me frequently to ask for money so that Natasha could eat and keep up her health and that of their unborn baby. There was no money for Natasha and Chaco to have their baby born in a clinic or hospital; there was no money for ultrasounds or any other care that pertains to the birth of a healthy child. In Haiti, approximately fifty-four out of every one thousand babies die at birth. At the same time, Haiti has the highest maternal mortality rate in the Western Hemisphere. Approximately six hundred and seventy Haitian women die out of every one hundred thousand due to pregnancy-related complications. Most of these deaths could be prevented if medical facilities were available to them. On the other hand, if facilities are available, most Haitian women cannot afford to use them.

Although the entrance fee for a medical facility ranges from twenty-five cents to sixty-four cents a day, most women cannot afford this. In most cases, these women are also expected to pay for everything from medical gloves to food.

Under the supervision of Natasha's grandmother, and by the light of burning candles, the baby boy was born in the tiny two-room concrete house. Her grandmother had delivered many babies in her lifetime – this was the norm in Haiti, especially when she was a younger woman.

I felt particularly attached to this child since one of his many names is my name. By the next morning, I was quite concerned and brought my thermometer over to take the baby's temperature. He had a slight fever and was fully dressed and wrapped in a blanket. The heat in the tiny house was intense, so I sponged him with a damp cloth, trying to keep the beads of sweat off his tiny forehead. Natasha had been feeding the baby drops of milk that dripped from a small water bag with a tiny pierced hole in the corner. I gave Chaco some money to please locate some drinking water.

When I poured the bottled water into the bag and started letting drops fall into the baby's mouth, the family was alarmed. They did not understand why the baby would drink anything but milk. When I picked him up and held him over my shoulder, people gasped. The word had spread that I was there. About five or six older ladies appeared in the house to observe. They were upset and ranting at Chaco and Natasha about something. They were upset that I had been giving the baby water. Chaco sent one of the younger children to go and fetch someone in the village that could speak English.

Apparently, it is Haitian custom to keep a baby horizontal for the first few months of life. Therefore, the older women were mortified when I put him over my shoulder and then proceeded to walk around the room. I tried to explain that it was part of our culture to give the baby water and hold him in various positions, especially when burping. They would have no part of what I had to say and continued to give me angry looks.

Later that day, Chaco and Natasha took the baby to Cap-Haïtien, where there is a medical clinic. Fortunately, he was put in the care of an American doctor. Baby Frank Robert Sandro was diagnosed with pneumonia. The American doctor sent them to a proper hospital an hour and a half away in the town of Milot because there was not adequate medicine and oxygen in his clinic.

Chaco and Natasha spent ten days in the hospital with their baby. Natasha slept in a chair and Chaco on the floor for the duration. Neither food nor water was available at the hospital for the baby or themselves, so Chaco would leave during the day to go out on the streets and desperately try to find something for them to eat or money for them to purchase formula for the baby. Natasha's milk had long since dried up because food had been scarce throughout her pregnancy and after the birth. Her diet consisted of rice and beans when they were available. In the hospital, they went days without eating, unless other people who were more fortunate took pity on them.

When it was time for the family to return home, they were handed a bill of 250 US dollars. The hospital told the couple that medical services were over. However, they were not allowed to leave the premises until the bill was paid. Natasha had to stay with the baby at the hospital while Chaco, once again, headed to the streets to earn money. He asked me if it was possible that anyone in Canada would be able to help them pay their bill. Chaco, Natasha, Baby Frank Robert Sandro, and I will be forever grateful to the graciousness and goodwill of the person who sent them the money.

DIARRHEA DILEMMA

IT SEEMS THAT every trip from Haiti to the Dominican Republic brings a different set of circumstances to overcome! One such occasion was the time I like to refer to as the diarrhea dilemma.

Dania and I arose at 6:00 a.m. to say our final farewells to the people in the village before departing in a tap tap at eight o'clock. At this point, I felt relatively well except for the deep sadness I felt having to say good-bye to those I loved in Fort Liberte. After our farewells around the village, the usual entourage of people accompanied us to the border in the tap tap, and we headed for Ouanam in the once again.

Alex was not allowed to leave Haiti this time and travel with us through the DR because his visa had expired, so Dania and I would be on our own for the bus trip across the Dominican Republic to the airport. Alex always looked after the red tape when it came to getting us out of one country and into the other in whichever direction we were travelling. On this particular moment, as we stood at the immigration hut on the Haitian side of the border, a sharp pain travelled through my stomach. Next came an overwhelming sensation of needing the toilet, and quickly! I tapped Alex as he was speaking in Creole to the lady in the hut. He paid no attention to me. "Alex!" I cried. "Please ask her where a bathroom is!" It turned out that there was a wooden shed some hundred yards away behind the immigration hut. This small shed was built from old signs and pieces of wood that were salvaged from one place or another. The door was a hanging piece of plywood that did not close all the way. Inside stood a toilet and a urinal; obviously the bathroom was coed!

At this point, the appearance of the bathroom didn't really matter. The toilet lid was down and after lifting it up, I knew why – there was no running water in the shed and the interior of the toilet was full. The stench immediately made me start to gag. The stench from the toilet burned my nostrils. I had no choice but to sit by now. I slowly lowered my bottom onto the seat of the toilet, praying that I would not touch its contents. I couldn't breathe. Gasping for fresh air, I pulled my shirt up over my head, hoping in some way it might work as a gas mask. After calming my breathing with my head in my shirt, I realized that the cheeks of my bottom were resting in a wet, warm, and mushy mess. I finished the job of filling the toilet to its maximum capacity. My stomach was feeling much relieved, and I scoured for some toilet paper. Just then the door swung open, and a man came in to use the urinal right beside me. "Bonjour," he said, as he proceeded to pee while I sat there in my dilemma. If I had spoken enough Creole, I would have asked him to find me something to wipe and clean the frosted cheeks of my behind.

As it was, he zipped up and said good-bye as we passed one another a smile. Once again, I scoured the shed to find something to clean myself with. I thought frantically, trying to come up with some smart solution or improvisation. Much time had passed, I was sure. All the girls and guys in our group must be wondering what was taking me so long, since we had a bus to catch in Dajabón to get us to the airport in Santiago for the three o'clock flight back to Toronto.

There was a yellow-lidded plastic trash pail beside me, and I had succumbed to the fact that this was my last resort for cleaning. I slowly slid the lid off to assess the contents. A swarm of flies buzzed inside among the well-used pieces of toilet paper. The odor in the room grew even stronger, and I lifted my shirt over my head again just enough that my eyes could see. I slowly picked up pieces of used paper and examined them to see which ones had the largest clean corners that I could tear off. This I found to be more horrific than actually sitting in what I was sitting in at the moment. I knew that it was going to take quite a lot of clean corners to fix the mess I was in. I examined and ripped until I was satisfied that I had enough paper. I used them sparingly, knowing that there was a lot to clean, and it wasn't all mine. I had to stand up to complete the task since there was no room for wiping when the toilet was so full. I approached the task systematically and diligently, all the while hoping that no one else would walk in. There was, of course, nowhere for washing my hands, but I figured that that was the least of my worries now. Feeling better and cleaner, I pulled up my shorts and proceeded out of the hanging door. The others were off in the distance waving at me. Alex, of course, was pointing to his watch, yelling, "Come on, Mom, you have a plane to catch!" As I approached them, another sharp pain tore through my stomach. There was no other option, I had to turn around and reenter the shed.

Of all the trips from Haiti to the Dominican interior, there are three that will be ever present in my mind. Once you have crossed the border into Dajabón, the

DR army is prevalent everywhere, checking papers of the Haitian people to assure that they are in the country legally. When you travel on the buses that run east from the border, there are random checkpoints every ten minutes or so run by the Dominican army. One or two men in uniform will board the bus and search for Haitians trying to illegally get into the DR. They walk up and down the aisles and either ask every Haitian for their papers or randomly pick a few who they feel may be suspicious. No one knows for sure whether these men in uniform are actual army officers or bandits and thieves dressed in army attire. Since they all carry a number of guns, no one is about to inquire or argue with them. On one such occasion, these men stopped our bus. Dania and I always become apprehensive when this happens since we are not accustomed to men swinging machine guns around or talking to passengers as if they were some lower class of human being. One of the men randomly chose a Haitian man and told him to get off with his luggage. The man did as they asked, and the men with guns got off right behind him. He was asked to show his papers, and it appeared to us that he did. We all peered out of the windows, afraid of what was to happen next. The man was asked to open his suitcase, and he did. It was a small old-style case with hard sides and flip-up latches. Inside, there appeared to be only articles of clothing and some toiletries. One of the men with guns started to rummage through the case. He picked up pieces of clothing and tossed them on the side of the road or into the brush behind him. When the suitcase was empty, the men with guns told him to empty his pockets, and he did. They took whatever he had then started to kick his suitcase around like a soccer ball. After a few minutes of these men degrading this poor Haitian and taking his belongings, they told the bus driver to move on. As the bus moved forward, Dania and I fought back feelings of anger and tears. Horror was in our hearts.

What would become of the man left standing on the side of the road?

On another occasion as we travelled from the border into the Dominican Republic, we were stopped at a checkpoint. Once again, men with machine guns entered the bus and searched for proper paperwork. As this was happening, I noticed an old pickup truck in front of us had also been stopped. Inside was a Haitian family. The back of the truck was piled very high with white sacks of rice. The younger people in the family sat up on top of the heap. I assumed that the family had harvested their rice crop and was bringing it into the Dominican Republic to sell since growing rice is in the preliminary stages of becoming a commodity for Haiti. The family members were told to exit the truck and stand on the side of the road. Other men in uniforms appeared with pitchforks. They jumped onto the heap of rice sacks and started stabbing. Rice started pouring out of the sacks.

It took me a while to realize that they were looking for stowaway Haitians in or among the sacks of rice. It was extremely hard to look, fearing that a spew of blood may appear among the white of the rice. The men stabbed and stabbed until they were satisfied that either the family's rice profits were ruined or there were no stowaways. By the vengeful way they attacked the sacks, I think they were probably let down that no one was hidden there. All I know is, if there was a Haitian person among the rice, he or she would be dead.

DON'T MESS WITH THE WHITE WOMAN

AFTER SPENDING CHRISTMAS vacation in Haiti, Dania and I were returning to the DR to catch our flight home. Denis was travelling with us on his way back to Santiago to return to university. Because he attends medical school in the Dominican Republic, he is savvy to the Dominican culture. He always knows when to play the proper role with whatever situation confronts him and dresses according to Dominican styles so that he is less likely to be a victim of racism.

On this occasion, the three of us were on the bus, Dania and I seated together and Denis alone, across the aisle. Once again, our bus was stopped by uniformed men carrying AK-47s. They asked all Haitians for paperwork. When they received Denis's, they seemed to read it for an exceptionally long time. His papers stated that he was attending university and studying to be a doctor. He was questioned about how he, a Haitian, could possibly afford to go to university. Denis explained that he had some very generous friends in the United States. He was asked if these friends had sent any money lately. He replied that they had not. He was asked if they paid for the fine clothes he was wearing because he was not dressed like a Haitian. He replied that they did not. The men then told Denis to get off the bus. At the time, I did not know what the men were saying to him since they were speaking Spanish. Consequently though, when we saw Denis rise and walk toward the door, Dania and I became frantic. I could tell that Denis had been asked to empty his pockets as I watched out the window. The bus driver was told to open the storage area of the bus and retrieve Denis's luggage. Now my heart was about to burst through my chest. One of the men told Denis to open the suitcase as he hit him with the butt end of his gun. More papers were handed over along with all his money.

I flew off the bus in a rage! A Dominican gentleman that was nearby came running over yelling at me to get back on the bus. "Like bloody hell," I replied, as I realized that he was speaking English. I begged him to tell me what was happening to Denis. He said that it was not my concern, and I should get back on the bus. I pleaded with the man, explaining my friendship with Denis. He explained to me that they had taken Denis's identification and other crucial papers. They were accusing him of being a spy because he did not look or act like a Haitian. Again, they were hitting Denis with their guns. They were bribing Denis for money. They told him that spies go to jail or to the sugarcane fields to cut cane till they die. They told him that if he wanted his passport and papers back that he was to come up with some money – possibly he could phone his rich American friends and tell them to send money.

I approached the scene, and all the while, Denis was telling me to get back on the bus. I told Denis that I knew what was going on. The two punks in uniform were giggling, assuming I was his older lover or paid companion. My cheeks were burning, and my head grew dizzy. I felt out of control with anger. A rush of adrenaline took over my body and my senses. I grabbed one of the men with the guns by the throat with my right hand. I made a fist with a pointed finger with the other. I stared at that bastard face to face and punched him in the chest. I was livid and out of control with anger. They changed their smirks into looks of fear as they stepped back from the crazy white lady. I ranted in anger at the top of my lungs, advancing toward them as they stepped backward. My pointed finger was now in his face, and I told Denis and Dania to get back on the bus.

"Okay, lady! Okay, lady!" the man with the gun replied. "Sorry, lady, sorry! Please get back on the bus with your friends!" So we did!

PERSPECTIVE

F OR DANIA AND I, leaving Haiti was the hardest moment in both our lives. Leaving Haiti was actually harder than watching our friends struggle in their deplorable situations. I know this sounds like an extremely selfish thing to say; it is hard to explain the feelings that come over us when we live with the Haitian people. The deep compassion we have for them grows constantly as we lived and breathed their culture. The bond between us is very strong. However, I realize that the family and friends in Fort Liberte were partially happy to have us there because we had some money in our pockets. I also realize that not all the relationships we had made were genuine. Some were just for the prospect of eating that day or receiving money. But what I do know for sure is that the good far outweighs the bad.

All the materialism of our world had disappeared. We were no longer just going through the motions each day; we were living life. With nothing in our hands, we were living life to the fullest. We no longer cared about our appearances and our bank accounts. What we did care about was the conversations we were having in the morning as we helped Olrich wash all the dishes from the day before. We cared about the fact that we were walking down the street with linked arms or holding hands with others, something that is never done in North America. We cared about the fact that instead of watching television or playing video games in the evening, we were on the street dancing, singing, or playing games, and no one was embarrassed to join in. Everyone participates no matter their age or gender.

Travelling to Haiti brought out a different person in both my husband and my son for the short time that they were there. For the first time, I heard my husband sing as he tried to teach an English game to a crowd of children gathered around him. Even with the language barrier, he was able to connect with the spirit of these children and their overwhelming eagerness to learn.

I watched my son, Braeden, always eager to lend a helping hand with the building of the house. I watched him get up and dance in a large circle of people. He tried to make them laugh and succeeded very well. I watched him as he piggybacked the children when they were too tired to walk and held little Duchana on his lap while she slept for hours so that she wouldn't have to sleep on the ground.

FAREWELL, HAITI

ON THE MORNINGS of our return to Canada, they are all there. Family and friends are gathered at the entrance of our building, waiting for us to come down. Tears have already started for us as we gaze one more time into the faces that have taught us so much about life. A tap tap waits and our luggage is tied to the top, fewer suitcases than when we arrived since most of what we brought has been given away. We make our way down the line, exchanging hugs, kisses, and farewells. Pierre Zulie is always the last as she waits with the fancy package of tablet she has made for us. It is her way of expressing her gratitude. She has memorized the words in English to ask me once again to send money when I can. I tell her as always that I will try.

Once again, anyone who can fit in the tap tap is allowed to make the trip to the border. There is none of the usual camaraderie on this tap tap ride; it is extremely quiet and heads are hung low. As I glance around, I see teary eyes in grown men. As we approach Ouanaminthe and the border, everyone starts to cling to each other; Dania and I are barely able to contain ourselves.

As we walk toward the border gate, I can see the green of the Dominican Republic on the other side. It is just steps away, but it is a whole new world. Everyone stays by our side while Alex gets us through customs and immigration. The gate is armed with guards with machine guns. We always make a final plea with the Dominican border guards to let our friends through to accompany us to the bus stop on the other side. Our plea never works.

As we are rushed through the metal gate in the Dominican Republic, we glance back into Haiti. It is barren and brown. There is litter everywhere. I see a group of people on the other side still standing and watching as we walk out of their view. I hope they have seen our final farewell wave before we turned the corner.

The culture shock has hit us already. There is loud music on the streets now. There are bars, cafes, gas stations, and stores. All of a sudden, food and drinks are everywhere. The contrast of a few hundred feet is astonishing. There are people dressed in fine attire and vacationers laughing as they peer into shop windows. It seems congested, busy, and loud. Once again, I glance back but Haiti is out of sight.

Alex has purchased our bus tickets to the city of Santiago, and our luggage is already aboard. Dania and I sit stunned as we gaze out the window at the passing scenery. It is so different here, and it is going to be so much more different in Canada. I try to think about home, but it is hard. It is hard, but a glimmer of excitement starts to come over me as I think about my home, husband, son, other daughter Michaela, and our pets. I try to focus on home, but Haiti still creeps into my thoughts. The one thought that stands out the most for me is *I need Haiti more than Haiti needs me!*

EPILOGUE

FROM THE FIRST time I travelled in Haiti with Alex, I was hooked. There is no part of my being that wasn't moved emotionally by the experience. I was forever changed. I knew that I would continue to return to this place for the rest of my life.

After spending time with the Haitian people, I learned to love them and their culture. I was faced with a new purpose in life. This purpose was and still is "How can I help these people?"

The living conditions that these human beings endure are deplorable. They live without the right to a drink of clean water or a meal each day. This is the year 2012, and they are bathing in basins of filth-ridden water and using buckets or holes in the ground as toilets. Once again, this is the year 2012, and Haitians live without electricity to light their homes and streets. They cook on charcoal, using makeshift stoves. Children cannot attend school, because there is no money. Adults cannot work because there are no jobs or infrastructure. Haitians cannot go to the doctor for medical care since doctors and medicine are scarce and money is obsolete. Too many die because they can't get simple antibiotics for an infection. We must remember that they are our neighbors, only four hours away by plane, and we must not forget them. Some people believe that terrible things happen there because Voodoo exists in rural places. If more people would do research about Haitian culture, they would discover that the majority of the population is Christian.

I have travelled there eight times and found Haitians to be an optimistic, loving people with a wonderful sprit. Perhaps we could learn a lesson from them and return to the most important things that life has to offer. Their life is not about what they have; it is about cherishing those they are with and what they can share on a daily basis.

INDEX

A

aftershocks, 67-68, 71
Alex, 7, 9-10, 13-14, 37-40, 47, 49, 67-68, 71-72, 74-76, 78, 80-81, 83-86, 89, 94-95, 102-3
Alexander, 9
Andy, 28, 30, 57, 63-66, 68
Atlantic Ocean, 60-61

B

beach, 9-10, 32, 61-62, 71, 73
beans, 21, 27, 30, 59, 69, 72, 80-81, 93
beer, 35, 51
board games, 72
border, 12, 14-15, 45, 74, 94-96, 102
Braeden, 45, 47-48, 101
bulldozer, 5, 88-90
bus, 9, 11-12, 38, 75-80, 86-89, 95-96, 98-99

C

camaraderie, 15, 66, 102
Canada, 15, 45, 59, 66, 68, 81, 89, 93, 102-3
canal, 58
candles, 10, 29, 58, 66, 75, 91
candy, 13, 19, 28, 72
Cap-Haïtien, 5, 43, 56, 59-60, 75, 77, 86, 93
Chaco, 56-60, 75-76, 80-82, 89, 91-93
charcoal, 31-34, 58, 69, 75, 77, 82, 105
Citadel, 5, 51, 54-55
city, 57, 60, 75, 80-83, 103
coffins, 57
cooking, 10, 15, 27, 32, 54, 66, 69, 71, 77, 82
cooking stoves, 26, 54
Creole, 9, 78, 84, 94-95
culture, 16, 80, 93, 100, 105
customs, 14, 102

D

Dania, 9-11, 13-18, 21-23, 28-29, 33, 45, 47-48, 51-52, 56-57, 60-61, 64, 94, 96, 98-100, 102-3
deforestation, 31-32
Demostene, 47-48
Denis, 49-50, 67, 98-99
diarrhea, 5, 94
disco, 35-36

107

dogs, 18
Dominican Republic, 9, 13, 38-39, 49, 67, 74, 94, 96, 98, 102
drinking water, 20, 69, 92
Duchana, 40, 101
Duchanse, 40

E

earthquake, 67, 71, 79, 82-83
education, 40-41, 49-50, 85
electricity, 10, 19, 29, 51, 58, 65, 71, 105
English, 41, 43

F

fish head, 21-23
Florica, 41
food, 15, 21-23, 27, 30, 32, 36, 59-60, 64, 67, 69, 77, 80-81, 84, 93
Fort Liberte, 16, 18-19, 24-25, 27, 29-32, 34, 38, 45, 49, 60-61, 63, 65, 75, 80, 86
Fort Liberte Bay, 24, 61, 78
Frances, 40-41
Franz, 9-10
Fredly, 40
french toast, 33-34
fridge, 59, 81-82

G

games, 10, 16, 24-25, 29, 52, 71-72
garbage, 13, 61, 71, 82
gifts, 61, 72
gourdes, 13-14, 20-21, 30, 32, 60, 74, 84
grapefruit, 61

H

Haiti, 7, 9-15, 30-34, 37-39, 47, 51, 57, 59-63, 67, 74-75, 77-81, 89-92, 94-96, 100, 102-3

Haitian music, 15, 64
Haitian women, 10
hospital, 11, 91, 93
hotel, 20, 37-39, 81
house, 5, 10, 21, 29, 31, 47, 55, 61, 65-69, 75, 77, 79-80, 93, 101
household, 15, 30, 66

I

ice, 51

J

Jason, 45-46
John, 55

L

laundry, 14, 25, 58, 66
Louvence, 41
love, 15-16, 33, 41, 48, 105

M

marshmallows, 33
Maurice, 39
Miami, 79, 85
milk, 34, 92
Milot, 5, 51-52, 93
Mitziel, 41
MOJAD, 5, 7, 63-64
money, 11, 27, 31-32, 34, 38, 41, 43-44, 49-51, 56, 63-64, 66-67, 91, 93, 99-100, 105
movies, 28-30
mud cakes, 84
music, 10, 35, 63, 76, 80, 86

N

Natasha, 91-93
nausea, 13, 22, 54

Nerlange, 39, 41
NGOs, 49, 66, 81-82

O

ocean, 60-62, 78
odors, 13, 65, 71, 83
orphanage, 5, 7, 71-73
Ouanaminthe, 14-15

P

paperwork, 96, 98
peanuts, 28
pesos, 13, 75
Peter, 87, 89
pikliz, 30, 87
Port-au-Prince, 5, 67, 74-77, 79-80, 82, 86-87, 89, 91
power company, 65
Punta Cana, 9, 37-38

R

Reneau, 9-10, 73, 77
restaurant, 59-60
rice, 16, 27, 30, 39, 43, 58-59, 69, 72, 77, 80-81, 93, 96-97
road, 15, 18, 57-58, 60, 77, 79, 88-89
Ron, 45
rum, 35, 51

S

Santiago, 5, 11, 95, 98, 103

school, 31, 37-38, 41, 43, 45-47, 49-50, 56-59, 63, 67, 75, 91, 105
ship, 61

T

tablet, 28, 102
tap tap, 14-17, 19, 51, 56-58, 60, 75-76, 80, 86, 94, 102
tent city, 79, 83-84
tents, 79, 82-84
torro, 35, 51
traffic, 57, 77, 80-82
trees, 25, 31, 53-54, 68, 77
turtle, 32

U

United Nations, 17, 19, 40, 65-66, 75

W

water, 14, 19-20, 27, 51-53, 58, 61, 65, 69, 71-72, 83, 85, 93, 95, 105
water bags, 69
wheelbarrows, 12-13, 27, 32
Willen, 75-76, 79-83, 89
Wisly, 43-44

Z

Zulie, Pierre, 21, 26, 28, 37-39, 41, 45, 47, 56, 65, 67-69, 75, 91, 102

Copyedited and indexed by Jan Denn D. Arriba
Reviewed by Stephanie Ernestine E. Salera

CPSIA information can be obtained at www.ICGtesting.com
Printed in the USA
BVOW08*1600120114

341552BV00001B/1/P

9 781479 763801